THE GRANDCHILD
I HOLD IN MY HEART

Recovery for Estranged Grandparents
and A Compassionate Guide to
Grief, Hope, and Unseen Loss.

NICCI BROCHARD
&
DR. BEN CHUBA

THE GRANDCHILD I HOLD IN MY HEART

Recovery for Estranged Grandparents
and A Compassionate Guide to
Grief, Hope, and Unseen Loss.

CROSSBORDER

New York, London, Quebec

CONTENTS

INTRODUCTION

When Love Is Silenced but Never Gone

For many grandparents, the pain of estrangement from a beloved grandchild is an invisible wound. It's a sorrow that remains largely unspoken, a loss that isn't always recognized by those around them. When the bond between grandparent and grandchild is severed, the emotional turmoil that follows can be overwhelming—yet the grief is often left in the shadows, tucked away as family dynamics shift and change. *The Grandchild I Hold in My Heart* is a compassionate guide designed specifically for those experiencing the heartache of estrangement, offering support, validation, and a path to healing. This book shines a light on the complex emotions of estranged grandparents, acknowledging the silent suffering they endure while providing a roadmap for recovery, hope, and eventual peace.

The pain of estrangement is multifaceted. For many grandparents, it feels as though a vital part of their heart is missing. The bond between them and their grandchild may have been one of deep affection, filled with laughter, shared memories, and unconditional love. To have that bond severed can feel like the loss of a piece of one's identity and sense of purpose. Yet, this pain often remains hidden from view. Family members and friends may be unaware of the heartache, and in many cases, the estranged grandparents may feel pressured to grieve in silence. There are no public rituals of mourning for this kind of loss, and the sorrow remains largely unseen by the world. It's a grief that doesn't come with a clear beginning or end, and it is often marked by unanswered questions, unresolved pain, and the feeling that there is no space to express the depth of loss.

This book acknowledges that pain. It offers validation for those who feel the deep ache of losing a grandchild, whether through physical distance, emotional estrangement, or strained family dynamics. The hurt is real, even though it may not always be recognized or supported by others. The silence surrounding this type of grief can make it feel isolating, but this guide aims to create a space where that pain is recognized and heard.

As you journey through the pages of *The Grandchild I Hold in My Heart*, you will explore the emotional arc that estranged grandparents often experience. The journey of healing begins with understanding the causes of estrangement—whether due to family conflict, misunderstandings, or external factors—and acknowledging the feelings of anger, sadness, and confusion that often accompany it. The book will then guide you through the emotional stages of grief: the initial shock, the longing for reconciliation, the acceptance of what cannot be changed, and the ultimate path to healing.

Grief is not a linear process, and the road to healing is often winding and full of setbacks. However, this book emphasizes that healing is possible, even in the face of profound loss. It doesn't promise that the pain will disappear, but it offers practical tools and exercises to help you process your grief in a healthy and constructive way. Mindfulness techniques, journaling prompts, and strategies for self-care are woven throughout the chapters to provide emotional support as you work through your sorrow. Along the way, you will find that healing doesn't mean forgetting the past; it means learning to carry the love you have for your grandchild in a way that allows you to move forward with hope.

Ultimately, *The Grandchild I Hold in My Heart* is about finding hope and peace, even in the midst of profound grief. It is a reminder that the love you feel for your grandchild cannot be erased or silenced, even if the relationship is currently distant. Love, though sometimes buried beneath layers of pain and misunderstanding, is never gone. This book will help you reconnect with that love, honor the memory of what once was, and create space for healing in your heart.

In the following chapters, you will find not only compassion for your pain but also a renewed sense of hope. While the road may be long and filled with challenges, it is possible to find a place of peace, joy, and reconnection. Whether your estrangement is temporary or permanent, *The Grandchild I Hold in My Heart* offers the tools and emotional support needed to heal and find a renewed sense of purpose. You are not alone in your grief, and your love for your grandchild will never truly fade. Let this book be your companion on the journey back to healing and hope.

PART I
THE QUIET HEARTBREAK

CHAPTER 1

INVISIBLE LOSS – THE GRIEF NO ONE TALKS ABOUT

Introduction

G rief is a deeply personal experience. It can manifest in a variety of ways, depending on the nature of the loss and the relationship that was formed. For most people, when they think of grief, they envision the loss of a loved one through death. However, there is another form of grief that often goes unrecognized and is seldom acknowledged: the grief of estrangement. Specifically, the pain felt by grandparents who are cut off from their grandchildren can be a complex, multifaceted sorrow that is invisible to others. This chapter will delve into the concept of "ambiguous loss" and "estrangement grief," shedding light on the unique emotional experience of being distanced from a grandchild and why society frequently overlooks this form of loss. Understanding these concepts is crucial for those who find themselves living through this painful reality, and it will help give voice to a grief that too often remains silent.

Defining "Ambiguous Loss" and "Estrangement Grief"

Before diving into the specific pain that estranged grandparents experience, it is important to understand the psychological concepts of ambiguous loss and estrangement grief.

Both of these terms help to explain the complexity and subtlety of the emotions involved in estrangement.

Ambiguous Loss

Ambiguous loss is a term first coined by Dr. Pauline Boss, a researcher and family therapist, to describe situations in which there is a loss without closure. Unlike death, where a person can mourn a clear and definitive end, ambiguous loss refers to situations where the lost relationship, person, or situation is undefined, unclear, or ongoing. It is often associated with losses that lack resolution, such as a missing person or an unresolved situation. Ambiguous loss is not just about the physical absence of someone but also the emotional or psychological absence.

When it comes to grandparents, ambiguous loss often occurs when they are cut off from their grandchildren. They may be physically alive but emotionally or psychologically distant, leading to confusion about the status of the relationship. It is as though the grandparent is left in a state of limbo, not knowing whether the loss is permanent, temporary, or what it truly signifies. There is no funeral, no ritual of closure, just the quiet and unsettling absence of the loved one who was once an integral part of their lives.

Estrangement Grief

Estrangement grief, on the other hand, refers specifically to the grief that stems from being cut off from a close family member or loved one. It is a grief that is often complicated by the feelings of rejection, abandonment, and confusion. In the context of estranged grandparents, this grief is marked by the deep emotional ache of being distanced from a grandchild. What makes estrangement grief unique is that it is a grief without closure— there is no certainty about why the relationship has ended or whether it will ever be repaired. The emotional pain is often compounded by the fact that grandparents may not fully understand the reasons behind the estrangement. In many cases, the distance may be a result of conflict with the parents of the grandchildren or other family members, leaving the grandparent feeling helpless and unable to fix the situation.

The pain of estrangement grief is often silent. It is not a grief that can be easily shared with others, as there is often a stigma attached to it. Many grandparents may feel embarrassed or ashamed to talk about the loss, fearing that they will be judged or dismissed. They may also feel isolated, as others may not fully understand the depth of the pain involved. This makes estrangement grief particularly difficult to cope with, as it often goes unacknowledged both by the larger society and within the family unit itself.

The Unique Pain of Being Cut Off from a Grandchild

Now that we have defined the terms of ambiguous loss and estrangement grief, we can begin to explore the specific pain that grandparents experience when they are cut off from their grandchildren. The bond between a grandparent and a grandchild is unique, often characterized by unconditional love, emotional support, and a sense of connection that transcends time and distance. For many grandparents, this bond is one of the most cherished relationships in their lives.

When this bond is severed, the emotional impact can be devastating. It is not just the loss of a grandchild, but the loss of an important and fulfilling role in the family. For grandparents, being distanced from their grandchildren can feel like a loss of identity, as they may see themselves as a protector, mentor, and caregiver to the younger generation. The idea of not being able to provide love, guidance, or support to a grandchild can create a deep sense of sadness and grief.

The pain is compounded by the feelings of helplessness that often accompany estrangement. Grandparents may feel as though they have no power to repair the relationship or reach out to their grandchild. They may be caught in the middle of a family dispute or conflict, unable to communicate with the grandchild due to a breakdown in family dynamics. This feeling of helplessness can contribute to feelings of anger and frustration, as grandparents are left with little control over the situation.

Another unique aspect of estrangement from a grandchild is the ambiguity surrounding the loss. Unlike a death, where the finality of the situation is clear, estrangement leaves grandparents with constant uncertainty. They may wonder if the relationship is truly over, if reconciliation is possible, or if they will ever have the chance to see their grandchild again. The inability to move forward or gain closure can leave grandparents stuck in a cycle of emotional turmoil.

The estranged grandparent may also feel a deep sense of shame or guilt. In some cases, they may feel responsible for the estrangement, believing that something they did or did not do caused the break in the relationship. Even if they are not to blame, they may still carry the weight of self-blame, questioning their actions or wondering if they could have done something differently to avoid the estrangement. This feeling of guilt can be especially difficult to process, as it complicates the grieving process and makes it harder to heal.

Why Society Often Overlooks This Form of Loss

One of the key reasons why the grief of estranged grandparents often goes unnoticed is that society tends to overlook or undervalue the importance of grandparent-grandchild relationships. In many cultures, the role of the grandparent is seen as secondary or even peripheral when compared to the roles of parents. Society often places more focus on nuclear family dynamics—parents, children, and immediate family—while sidelining the contributions and emotional significance that grandparents bring to the family unit.

Additionally, there is a tendency in society to minimize the impact of estrangement. When family members become estranged, the focus is often placed on the immediate family, particularly parents and children, while the grief of extended family members, like grandparents, is dismissed or ignored. This creates an emotional vacuum for grandparents, who may feel that their grief is not valid or that they have no right to grieve the loss of a relationship that others may not view as significant. As a result, the pain of estrangement is often silenced, and grandparents are left to cope with their grief in isolation.

There is also the issue of stigma. Estrangement is often seen as a "family problem," something that should be dealt with internally rather than acknowledged in public or discussed openly. In some cases, grandparents may be reluctant to talk about their grief for fear of being judged or blamed. The feeling of shame can further isolate them, making it difficult for them to find support or validation for their emotions. This social silence around estrangement can exacerbate the pain, leaving grandparents feeling even more disconnected and unheard.

Finally, the complexity of estrangement grief can make it difficult for others to understand. Unlike other forms of loss, such as death or divorce, estrangement does not come with a clear ending. There is no closure, no funeral, and no official recognition of the grief. The lack of a public ritual of mourning makes it harder for others to recognize the pain involved, and for estranged grandparents, this lack of acknowledgment can be deeply painful.

Conclusion

Estrangement grief is one of the most challenging and often overlooked forms of loss. It is a silent grief, one that lacks the clear structure and public recognition that other forms of grief receive. For grandparents who are cut off from their grandchildren, the pain is deep and multifaceted. It is a grief born of confusion, helplessness, and a profound sense of loss—one that often goes unnoticed by society.

In this chapter, we've explored the concepts of ambiguous loss and estrangement grief, defining them and explaining how they manifest in the lives of estranged grandparents. We've also examined the unique emotional toll that estrangement can take, both in terms of the pain of losing a grandchild and the additional burden of societal indifference. Understanding these concepts is the first step toward acknowledging the pain of estrangement and allowing the healing process to begin.

It is important for estranged grandparents to know that their grief is valid, that the pain they feel is real, and that they are not alone in their experience. While society may not always recognize this type of grief, there is support available for those who are willing to embark on the difficult but ultimately rewarding journey of healing. This chapter is just the beginning of that journey—one that will allow estranged grandparents to move from a place of pain and uncertainty toward one of understanding, acceptance, and hope.

CHAPTER 2

HOW DID THIS HAPPEN? – TRACING THE PATH TO ESTRANGEMENT

Introduction

The journey toward estrangement is seldom a simple, linear path. For grandparents, the road to being cut off from their grandchildren is often marked by complexity, misunderstandings, and a series of emotional, relational, and sometimes legal challenges. It can feel like an unexpected rupture that leaves grandparents blindsided, or a slow, painful unraveling that takes years to reach its breaking point. Understanding the underlying causes of estrangement is crucial in coming to terms with the situation, as it not only sheds light on the reasons for the distance but also helps to make sense of the seemingly incomprehensible emotions involved. In this chapter, we will explore the common causes of estrangement, including family conflicts, divorce, custody battles, and generational wounds. We will also delve into the roles that adult children, in-laws, and legal systems play in the estrangement process. Finally, we will examine the differing dynamics between sudden and gradual estrangement and how each scenario impacts the emotional journey of the grandparent.

Common Causes of Estrangement

Estrangement from grandchildren does not happen in a vacuum; it is often the result of a confluence of family dynamics, emotional conflicts, and external forces. While each estrangement story is unique, there are several common causes that can help explain why a grandparent might find themselves distanced from their grandchildren.

1. Family Conflict

Family conflict is one of the most common and profound causes of estrangement. These conflicts can arise from many different sources, including personality clashes, ideological differences, or unresolved emotional issues between family members. Grandparents may become embroiled in these conflicts, either directly or indirectly, and may find themselves alienated as a result.

For example, a grandparent who has a strong relationship with their child may be caught in the middle of a dispute between that child and their spouse (the grandchild's parent). In some cases, one parent may forbid the grandparent from seeing the grandchildren due to tensions with their own parents. Such conflicts can be difficult for grandparents to navigate, especially when they feel emotionally torn between supporting their child and maintaining their relationship with their grandchild. The emotional complexities involved in family conflict can lead to misunderstandings and miscommunications, which in turn can escalate into estrangement.

2. Divorce and Custody Issues

Divorce is another major factor that can contribute to estrangement between grandparents and grandchildren. When parents divorce, the lives of everyone involved are disrupted, and the emotional and logistical repercussions often extend to the extended family. In many cases, grandparents find themselves caught in the crossfire of custody battles, with one parent seeking to limit contact with the other side of the family.

Custody issues can become particularly tricky when there is disagreement over who will have access to the grandchildren. If a grandparent's child (the parent of the grandchild) is not granted primary custody or visitation rights, the grandparent may lose contact with their grandchildren due to the limitations placed on the custodial parent's ability to facilitate those relationships. In these cases, a grandparent's estrangement is often more about the legal constraints on the family's dynamics than personal conflict, though the emotional consequences can be just as profound.

Additionally, when grandparents take sides in a divorce—whether actively or passively—it can strain their relationship with the estranged family member. If one parent feels that their side of the family is unsupportive or has taken the other parent's side, it can lead to further isolation and, in some cases, a complete severing of ties.

3. Generational Wounds

Generational wounds refer to the emotional scars passed down from one generation to another. These wounds can take the form of unresolved conflicts, unhealthy relationship patterns, or unaddressed trauma that affects how family members interact. In the context of estranged grandparents, generational wounds often arise when the grandparent's relationship with their own child (the parent of the grandchild) has been strained or difficult.

For example, a grandparent may have had a contentious relationship with their child when they were growing up, and those unresolved issues may carry over into the grandparent-child relationship once that child becomes a parent. The child may feel resentment toward their parent and, as a result, may choose to limit or sever contact between the grandparent and their grandchild. In these situations, the grandparent becomes an unwilling participant in a generational cycle of emotional pain and disconnection, with no clear resolution or closure in sight.

4. External Influences

Sometimes, estrangement is the result of external influences that exert pressure on family relationships. These can include the involvement of in-laws, new spouses, or even the influence of social media and online platforms. For example, a grandparent may experience estrangement due to the influence of an in-law or new partner who has a negative opinion of them or their role in the family. In such cases, the in-law may create friction or exert pressure on the parent (the grandchild's parent) to cut ties with the grandparent. External influences, especially when they come from a new or outside source, can create feelings of isolation and confusion for the grandparent.

The Roles of Adult Children, In-Laws, and Legal Systems

The roles of adult children and in-laws are pivotal in the estrangement process, as they often hold the power to determine the level of access grandparents have to their grandchildren. While many grandparents try to maintain a neutral and supportive role, the relationships with their adult children and in-laws can have a significant impact on the dynamics between them and their grandchildren.

1. Adult Children

Adult children are at the heart of most grandparent-grandchild estrangements, as they are the gatekeepers to the relationship. When a grandparent becomes estranged from a grandchild, it is often due to a breakdown in the relationship with their own child (the grandchild's parent). A variety of reasons can contribute to this breakdown, including disagreements, differences in parenting styles, or even deep-seated emotional issues from the past.

A parent may choose to limit or cut off access to the grandparent if they feel that the grandparent has overstepped boundaries, criticized their parenting choices, or played a disruptive role in the family. Alternatively, the parent may distance themselves from the grandparent if they perceive that the grandparent has caused emotional harm or acted inappropriately in the past. In these cases, the parent's decision to limit contact with the grandparent is typically a reflection of their own emotional state, frustrations, or conflicts.

2. In-Laws

In-laws, particularly the spouse of the adult child, can also play a significant role in the estrangement process. A grandparent may experience tension or conflict with their child's spouse, which can create a barrier to access to the grandchildren. In-laws may harbor resentment or have negative feelings toward the grandparent, either due to past experiences or because of differing expectations about family roles.

The influence of an in-law can sometimes lead to one parent feeling forced to take sides, especially if they feel pressure from their spouse to align with their perspective. In some cases, this dynamic can lead to the estrangement of the grandparent, even if the conflict is not directly with the grandparent themselves.

3. Legal Systems

Legal systems also play a crucial role in grandparent-grandchild estrangement, particularly in cases of divorce or custody battles. When parents are involved in legal disputes over custody, visitation, or child support, grandparents can find themselves caught in the middle, with little recourse for maintaining contact with their grandchildren. Many grandparents are unable to assert their right to visitation without going through complex legal processes, and even then, success is not guaranteed.

In some jurisdictions, grandparents may have the legal right to request visitation if they can demonstrate that their relationship with the grandchild is in the child's best interest. However, these legal battles are often expensive, emotionally taxing, and fraught with uncertainty. The involvement of the legal system can exacerbate the emotional pain of estrangement, making the experience even more challenging for grandparents.

When the Silence is Sudden vs. Gradual Estrangement

Estrangement can occur in a variety of ways, and the timeline of the estrangement process can significantly impact the emotional experience for grandparents. For some, the silence and distance come suddenly, with no warning or explanation. For others, estrangement is a gradual process, with the relationship slowly deteriorating over time until it eventually reaches a breaking point.

1. Sudden Estrangement

Sudden estrangement can feel like an emotional shock to the system. One day, grandparents may be actively involved in their grandchild's life—attending events, helping with childcare, and enjoying a close relationship—and the next, they are shut out with no clear explanation. This type of estrangement can be devastating because there is no opportunity for closure or preparation. Grandparents may feel blindsided by the sudden shift and struggle to understand what went wrong. In some cases, the estranged grandparent may not even be given an explanation, leaving them with a profound sense of confusion and helplessness.

The emotional impact of sudden estrangement is often intensified by the lack of a clear cause or reason. When grandparents are left in the dark about why the relationship ended, they may experience feelings of rejection, guilt, and self-blame. The uncertainty surrounding the estrangement can make it even harder to process the emotions involved, as there is no closure or resolution.

2. Gradual Estrangement

Gradual estrangement, on the other hand, can be equally painful, but the emotional journey tends to unfold more slowly. In cases of gradual estrangement, grandparents may notice subtle shifts in the relationship over time. At first, it may seem like a minor misunderstanding or a temporary issue, but over time, the distance grows. The grandparent may find that their calls are no longer returned, visits are postponed, and communication becomes less frequent. Gradual estrangement can feel like a slow unraveling, and the emotional pain builds over time as the relationship weakens.

The advantage of gradual estrangement, if there is one, is that it can give grandparents time to process the changes and attempt to address the issues that may be causing the distance. However, it can also make it harder to pinpoint the exact moment when the relationship began to fall apart. As a result, grandparents may find themselves questioning whether they missed signs or opportunities to mend the relationship. In some cases, they may feel like passive observers as the relationship slowly drifts away.

Conclusion

Estrangement from grandchildren is a complex and multifaceted process. While there are many different paths to estrangement, common causes often involve family conflict, divorce, custody battles, and generational wounds. Understanding the roles that adult children, in-laws, and legal systems play in this process is essential for making sense of the situation. Whether the estrangement is sudden or gradual, the emotional impact on grandparents is profound, and the pain of being cut off from a grandchild can leave lasting scars. By recognizing the underlying causes of estrangement, grandparents can begin to understand the emotional landscape they find themselves navigating and, ultimately, begin the process of healing.

GRANDPARENT LOVE – BONDS THAT RUN DEEPER THAN TIME

Introduction

In the grand tapestry of family relationships, the bond between grandparents and grandchildren is uniquely precious. It is a relationship that transcends the ordinary, often characterized by unconditional love, shared experiences, and a deep emotional connection that grows over time. For many grandparents, their grandchildren represent not only the joy of seeing the next generation blossom but also the fulfillment of a lifetime of wisdom, experiences, and love passed down. This chapter explores the emotional and developmental significance of the grandparent-grandchild relationship, offering a closer look at the unique role grandparents play in a child's life. We will also reflect on the joyful moments shared before the estrangement, remembering the richness of those experiences, and discuss how grandparents can hold onto love despite the absence of physical presence. Even when the relationship is strained or distant, the love between grandparent and grandchild remains strong, a bond that runs deeper than time.

The Emotional and Developmental Significance of the Grandparent-Grandchild Relationship

Grandparents hold a special place in the emotional and developmental development of children. While parents are responsible for providing the day-to-day care, guidance, and discipline, grandparents often serve as a source of unconditional love and emotional support. They are typically not burdened by the same responsibilities that parents face and, as a result, can offer a more relaxed, nurturing environment for their grandchildren. This difference in roles allows grandparents to develop a relationship with their grandchildren that is often characterized by a unique form of love and care—one that is filled with patience, understanding, and an absence of the day-to-day stresses that may affect parental relationships.

From a developmental perspective, the relationship between grandparents and grandchildren can have a significant impact on a child's emotional and social growth. Research has shown that strong grandparent-grandchild bonds can help foster a child's sense of security and belonging, which are fundamental for healthy emotional development. Grandparents often provide a steady source of support and comfort, offering a space where children can feel safe to express their feelings, explore their interests, and learn from life experiences. The emotional support grandparents provide can help buffer children from stress and adversity, giving them a sense of stability even when life around them is tumultuous.

The role of a grandparent often extends beyond that of a caregiver; they can be mentors, guides, and confidantes to their grandchildren. Whether through shared stories, activities, or simply offering a listening ear, grandparents help children navigate the complexities of life. Their wisdom—gained through years of experience—becomes a valuable resource for their grandchildren, teaching them important lessons about resilience, patience, and kindness. Moreover, grandparents often serve as a bridge between generations, helping children understand their cultural heritage, family history, and the legacy of their ancestors.

For many grandchildren, spending time with their grandparents is a source of immense joy and comfort. The love shared is often felt on a deep, emotional level, a love that remains with children throughout their lives. Even as children grow older and their relationships with their parents evolve, the bond with their grandparents remains a constant source of affection and security.

Sharing Stories of Joyful Times Before the Estrangement

Before the estrangement, there were likely countless moments of happiness and connection between grandparent and grandchild. These memories form the foundation of the relationship, and they are often cherished by both parties. For many grandparents, these memories are a source of comfort, even as they navigate the pain of estrangement. In the midst of the silence and distance, holding onto these joyful moments can provide a sense of continuity and connection to a past filled with love.

Grandparents often have the privilege of witnessing key moments in their grandchildren's lives—first steps, birthdays, graduations, and other milestones. These moments create an emotional bond that is difficult to break. The joy of seeing a grandchild grow, develop, and discover the world is a shared experience that remains etched in the hearts of both grandparents and grandchildren.

Think of the quiet afternoons spent reading stories together, the trips to the park, or the quiet moments of connection over a warm cup of tea. These are the memories that make the grandparent-grandchild relationship unique. It is often the simple, everyday moments that form the strongest emotional ties. Grandparents may remember the sound of their grandchild's laughter, the joy in their eyes during family gatherings, or the way their grandchild would run to them for comfort and reassurance. These are the moments that define the relationship and that continue to live on in the heart, even when physical presence is no longer possible.

During times of estrangement, it can be helpful for grandparents to focus on these memories as a way of preserving the love they share with their grandchildren. Reflecting on the good times before the estrangement can offer a sense of peace and remind grandparents of the deep emotional connection that still exists, even in the absence of physical contact. These memories serve as a reminder that the bond between grandparent and grandchild cannot be easily broken and that, regardless of the present circumstances, love endures.

While the pain of estrangement may cloud the present, these joyful memories can serve as a lifeline, reminding grandparents of the richness of the relationship that once was. It is through these memories that grandparents can hold on to the love they have for their grandchildren, even when they are not physically present in each other's lives.

Holding onto Love Without Physical Presence

One of the most difficult aspects of estrangement is the absence of physical presence. Grandparents may find themselves longing to hold their grandchild in their arms, to see them grow, to share in their triumphs and struggles. The absence can feel overwhelming, and the yearning for closeness is palpable. However, despite the physical distance, the emotional bond between grandparent and grandchild remains strong, even if it is not currently being expressed through regular visits or contact.

Holding onto love without physical presence requires a shift in perspective. It means understanding that love does not require constant physical proximity to be real or meaningful. Love is not confined to the space between two people, but rather it transcends time, distance, and circumstance. Even when a grandchild is not physically present, a grandparent's love for them continues to exist, stored in memories, thoughts, and feelings.

For many grandparents, the love they have for their grandchildren is a constant force—one that remains in their hearts even when the relationship is distant or strained. While the pain of estrangement can make it feel as though the love has been lost, it is important to recognize that love does not vanish. It continues to grow and evolve, even without the daily interactions that once defined the relationship.

One way to hold onto love without physical presence is through writing letters or keeping a journal. Grandparents may find solace in writing letters to their grandchildren, expressing their love, thoughts, and hopes for the future. These letters, even if never read, serve as a way of maintaining a connection and expressing emotions that may be difficult to articulate in other ways. Writing can also be a form of therapy, allowing grandparents to process their feelings, release their grief, and hold onto the love they continue to feel for their grandchildren.

Additionally, grandparents can hold onto their love by finding ways to honor the relationship, even from a distance. This could be through acts of kindness, prayers, or simply holding space in their hearts for the grandchild. The act of honoring the relationship, even in the absence of contact, affirms the enduring nature of the bond.

In some cases, grandparents may also find comfort in reaching out in non-intrusive ways—such as sending a card on special occasions or leaving a message that expresses love without expecting anything in return. These small gestures can keep the door open for future reconnection while demonstrating that the grandparent's love remains unwavering.

Conclusion

The bond between grandparents and grandchildren is one of the most powerful and enduring relationships in a family. It is a connection that goes beyond the simple roles of caregiver or family member; it is a relationship built on love, shared experiences, and mutual respect. The emotional and developmental significance of this bond cannot be overstated—it is a source of joy, comfort, and stability for children, and a wellspring of affection and pride for grandparents.

Even when estrangement occurs, the love between grandparent and grandchild does not fade. While the absence of physical presence can be difficult to bear, grandparents can continue to hold onto their love through cherished memories, writing, and small acts of kindness. The bond that runs deeper than time remains intact, and the love shared between a grandparent and their grandchild continues to exist, transcending the distance that may separate them. Through reflection, hope, and understanding, grandparents can keep the flame of love alive, even in the face of estrangement. The heart of a grandparent is never truly empty, for it always holds a place for the grandchild they love.

PART II
NAMING THE HURT, MAKING SPACE FOR HEALING

CHAPTER 4

A THOUSAND UNSENT CARDS – PROCESSING YOUR GRIEF

Introduction

Grief is a deeply personal and often messy experience. It doesn't follow a clear, linear path, and it certainly doesn't operate on anyone's timeline. For grandparents who have become estranged from their grandchildren, the process of grief can be especially complicated. This is a loss unlike any other—one that is marked by silence, ambiguity, and unresolved emotions. It can feel like there's a constant ache in your heart, and yet no one truly understands the depth of your pain. Perhaps the hardest part of this grief is the inability to express it—to articulate your love, your longing, your sorrow. This chapter is about processing that grief, giving voice to the feelings that may have been bottled up for far too long. We'll explore how journaling can become a therapeutic outlet, offering a space to express what might never be said aloud. We'll also dive into the complex emotions of sadness, anger, guilt, and helplessness that often accompany estrangement, and understand the stages of grief in the context of estrangement, providing a roadmap for the emotional terrain you might find yourself navigating.

Journaling Your Heartbreak: What You Would Say if You Could

When you're estranged from a grandchild, one of the hardest things is the silence. There's an overwhelming feeling that you can't speak your truth—either because the relationship is severed, or because you don't want to create further tension by reaching out. The emotions that come with this silence are profound and complex, and they can quickly overwhelm the heart and mind.

Journaling provides a private space to let these emotions flow without judgment, without worrying about how your words might be received. It's a way to articulate your grief, love, and confusion when there's no one else to listen. Journaling allows you to create a dialogue with yourself, a space where you can say all the things you wish you could express to your grandchild, whether they are ever read or not.

Consider starting by writing a letter to your grandchild. Imagine what you would say if you had the chance to communicate freely and without fear of rejection. What would you tell them about your love for them? What memories do you cherish the most? What would you ask them if you could speak to them, not as a grandparent caught in the web of estrangement, but as someone who simply wants to share their heart?

Perhaps your letter would be filled with words of apology, even if you don't feel like you're entirely at fault. Maybe you want to explain yourself, to offer insight into the circumstances that led to the estrangement. Or, your words might be filled with longing and love, expressing your wish to see them again, to hold them close, to share in the joy of their lives.

But journaling isn't just about writing letters. It's about letting your heart speak freely, allowing the grief to spill out in ways that might feel too painful to say aloud. You can express frustration, regret, and the overwhelming sense of loss that comes with estrangement. In many cases, the act of journaling allows you to release some of the emotional pressure that has been building up, offering a small degree of relief.

Through this process, you might find that writing helps you organize your thoughts and emotions. It can make the grief feel less chaotic and more understandable. You may begin to see patterns in your thoughts, areas where healing is possible, or moments when you can release old feelings that no longer serve you.

Navigating Complex Emotions: Sadness, Anger, Guilt, Helplessness

Grief is a mix of emotions, and for those experiencing estrangement from a grandchild, the emotional landscape is especially challenging. The silence can feel deafening, and the absence of the relationship leaves a void that nothing seems to fill. The pain can manifest in many forms—sadness, anger, guilt, and helplessness—and each of these emotions has its own set of complexities that make the grieving process difficult to navigate.

1. Sadness

Sadness is the most apparent emotion that comes with estrangement. It's a quiet sorrow that lingers, the kind that follows you in every moment, reminding you of the love you once shared with your grandchild. This sadness often has no immediate outlet. Unlike other forms of grief, where you can openly mourn, sadness due to estrangement is often isolated, as the relationship that is being mourned is not something that can be publicly grieved. It's the sorrow of missed birthdays, of never being there for milestones, of not being able to offer your support when your grandchild needs it most.

Sadness can also come from the realization that the person you once knew may be changing in ways you can no longer witness. Perhaps they are growing older, becoming a young adult, or navigating the world without the guidance or love you once provided. That feeling of being left behind can be incredibly painful.

2. Anger

Anger often arises when we feel wronged or rejected. When estranged from a grandchild, this anger may not just be directed at the child themselves, but at the circumstances, at other family members, or even at yourself. It might stem from feeling powerless in the situation or frustrated at not being able to fix what's broken. Perhaps you feel angry at the parents involved in the estrangement, at the way they've handled things, or at the dynamics that caused the rift. This anger may also turn inward, with feelings of self-blame creeping in. You might wonder, "Could I have done something differently?" or "Where did I go wrong?"

Anger is a natural response to feeling unjustly treated, and it is important to recognize that it is an emotion that demands attention. Suppressing anger can lead to further emotional turmoil, so it's crucial to acknowledge it and allow yourself to express it—whether through journaling, conversation, or another outlet that feels right for you.

3. Guilt

Guilt often accompanies estrangement, and for grandparents, it can be especially sharp. You may question whether you said the wrong thing, acted too harshly, or didn't do enough to maintain the relationship. It's common for grandparents to feel that they failed in some way, even when the estrangement was beyond their control. This can be compounded by feelings of inadequacy. You may worry that, as a grandparent, you weren't fulfilling the role you hoped for or that you could have done more to prevent the situation.

Guilt, like anger, can be a complicated emotion. While some amount of self-reflection can be helpful in understanding what went wrong, excessive guilt is often unwarranted. It's essential to differentiate between things within your control and things that were dictated by external circumstances. Recognizing that you can only control your own actions and responses, and not the actions of others, is a critical step in releasing unnecessary guilt.

4. Helplessness

Perhaps the most paralyzing emotion associated with estrangement is helplessness. The sense that you have no power to change the situation, no ability to fix what has broken, can leave you feeling immobilized. This feeling often arises when grandparents want to repair the relationship but are unsure how to do so. They may try to reach out, only to face rejection or silence, which reinforces the sense that nothing can be done.

Helplessness is particularly difficult because it often comes with the knowledge that, no matter how much love or care you give, you may not be able to change the circumstances. While this can be a painful realization, it's important to remember that healing is not always about fixing the relationship. Sometimes, it's about accepting the situation as it is and finding ways to care for your own heart, regardless of the outcome.

Understanding Stages of Grief Through the Lens of Estrangement

Grief is often described in terms of stages, with the most widely known model being Elisabeth Kübler-Ross's five stages: denial, anger, bargaining, depression, and acceptance. While not everyone will experience these stages in the same way or in the same order, they provide a helpful framework for understanding the emotional journey of grief. For estranged grandparents, these stages can look slightly different, shaped by the particular nature of estrangement. Here, we'll explore how these stages may manifest when the grief stems from being cut off from a grandchild.

1. Denial

In the denial stage, grandparents may refuse to accept the reality of the estrangement. They might convince themselves that things will get better, that the estrangement is just temporary, or that the relationship will soon be repaired. This stage is often filled with hope, even if it's unrealistic, and it can delay the grieving process.

2. Anger

As discussed, anger often surfaces when estrangement becomes undeniable. Grandparents may feel anger toward the parents or other family members involved in the estrangement. They may feel wronged, misunderstood, or rejected, and this anger can lead to frustration when they realize that they have no control over the situation.

3. Bargaining

During the bargaining phase, grandparents might search for ways to mend the relationship. They may reach out repeatedly, make compromises, or even try to change their behavior to meet the expectations of others in the family. Bargaining is often a sign of desperation, a desire to fix things, and a sense of feeling like they're doing everything they can to restore the relationship.

4. Depression

The depression stage is often characterized by profound sadness and despair. When grandparents realize that there is nothing they can do to repair the estrangement, they may feel an overwhelming sense of loss. This stage can also involve feelings of isolation and loneliness, as estranged grandparents may feel that no one truly understands the depth of their grief.

5. Acceptance

Acceptance comes when grandparents come to terms with the reality of the estrangement. This doesn't mean they've stopped loving their grandchild, but it means they've found a way to live with the loss. They may shift their focus toward healing, journaling, or finding support, and they may begin to find peace in knowing that they have done all they can.

Conclusion

The grief of estrangement is complex and multifaceted, often accompanied by a mix of sadness, anger, guilt, and helplessness. Processing this grief requires patience, self-compassion, and the willingness to confront painful emotions. Journaling can be a powerful tool in this process, offering an outlet for emotions that might otherwise remain trapped inside. By acknowledging and navigating these complex emotions, grandparents can begin to find healing and move toward acceptance—learning to live with the loss and ultimately finding a sense of peace. Though the road may be long and challenging, it's important to remember that the love shared between a grandparent and grandchild remains, even in the silence. Healing begins when you give yourself permission to grieve, express your feelings, and slowly rebuild your emotional well-being.

CHAPTER 5

BUT I WAS ALWAYS THERE – UNPACKING GUILT AND SELF-BLAME

Introduction

One of the most painful emotions that accompanies estrangement from a grandchild is guilt. It's a feeling that can permeate every thought, cloud every memory, and leave grandparents questioning themselves long after the distance has formed. For many grandparents, the bond with their grandchildren is a deeply cherished one, built on years of love, care, and devotion. So when the relationship is broken, the instinctive reaction is often one of self-blame—"What did I do wrong? Why wasn't I enough?" In this chapter, we will explore how grandparents often carry misplaced guilt in the wake of estrangement, and how to begin to differentiate between what is within your control and what is beyond it. Understanding where guilt is warranted and where it is unjustified is an important step in finding healing. Most importantly, we will discuss how to cultivate grace and self-compassion amidst the painful narrative of estrangement, so that grandparents can begin to release the weight of guilt and find a path toward peace.

How Grandparents Carry Misplaced Guilt

Guilt is a natural response when we feel we have failed in some way, and for many grandparents, estrangement from their grandchildren feels like a failure. However, the guilt that arises in these situations is often misplaced. The instinct to blame oneself for the rift is common, especially for grandparents who may have been a significant part of their grandchild's life up until that point. When things go wrong, it's easy to believe that somehow, you could have done more to prevent the situation, to bridge the gap, or to fix what was broken.

The truth, however, is that estrangement is rarely caused by a single action or fault. It is usually the result of a complex mix of family dynamics, miscommunications, emotional baggage, and sometimes, uncontrollable circumstances like divorce or conflict between the parents. It's important for grandparents to realize that they are often not the sole cause of the estrangement, even though the guilt they feel might suggest otherwise.

For example, many grandparents may carry guilt over a specific moment or event. They might replay a conversation, a disagreement, or an action that they believe led to the estrangement, and they may wonder if they could have acted differently. While it's natural to want to take responsibility for one's actions, it's important to recognize that the process of estrangement is rarely as simple as one instance. Often, it is the result of cumulative factors—things that were said, done, or left unsaid over time—that contributed to the breakdown of the relationship.

Furthermore, the role of external influences, such as other family members or the legal system, can significantly impact the situation. Many grandparents find themselves caught in the middle of larger family conflicts that they cannot control, such as a disagreement between parents, custody battles, or the influence of in-laws. In these situations, guilt is often a heavy burden that grandparents carry without reason. They may feel responsible for the rupture in the family, yet there is little they can do to change the outcome.

It's also worth acknowledging that some grandparents internalize guilt because they feel powerless in the situation. When estranged, it can feel like everything is out of their hands, and that they have no way to fix what has been broken. This sense of helplessness can often turn inward, with grandparents blaming themselves for the distance and feeling that they are the ones who have failed, rather than recognizing that some things are simply beyond their control.

Differentiating What You Can and Cannot Control

The first step in unpacking guilt and self-blame is recognizing what is within your control and what is not. When you are estranged from your grandchild, it can feel as though you are at the mercy of forces that you cannot influence. The truth is, no one can control another person's actions, and when it comes to family dynamics, there are many factors that are outside your influence. Understanding where your power lies is crucial for processing your grief and guilt in a healthy way.

1. What You Can Control

There are certainly aspects of the estrangement that you can control—most notably, your actions and your responses. The way you choose to handle the estrangement, the way you care for yourself through this process, and the way you respond to your family dynamics are all within your control. Even though the situation may feel overwhelmingly out of your hands, you still have the ability to make choices that promote healing and self-compassion.

For example, you can choose to reach out to your grandchild (if it's appropriate and safe to do so), you can choose to express your feelings in a healthy way (such as journaling, speaking with a counselor, or joining a support group), and you can choose to focus on your own emotional well-being. While you cannot force reconciliation or change the decisions of others, you can control how you navigate this period of your life and how you care for your own mental and emotional health.

Moreover, you can control the way you reflect on the past. While guilt may initially cloud your thinking, over time, you can choose to look back with a more balanced perspective. You may begin to see that while there were moments when things could have been handled differently, there were also times when you acted out of love and devotion. By shifting your focus from self-blame to self-reflection, you can give yourself the grace to recognize your role without taking on excessive guilt.

2. What You Cannot Control

There are, however, many aspects of the situation that are simply out of your control. For instance, you cannot control how other family members, especially the parents of your grandchild, behave or how they view your relationship with their child. If there has been conflict or miscommunication between you and your child or their spouse, it may be beyond your control to change their perspective. You may have done everything you could to maintain a strong bond with your grandchild, but ultimately, the decisions made by others will impact the relationship.

Additionally, external circumstances like divorce, custody issues, or family secrets may contribute to the estrangement, and these are factors that you cannot change. In some cases, the estrangement may be the result of a power struggle or control dynamics within the family, and no matter how much love or effort you put in, these larger forces will play a significant role in shaping the outcome.

Acknowledging that certain elements are beyond your control can help alleviate the pressure to "fix" things that are unfixable. Recognizing that some situations are not a reflection of your own failures, but rather the result of complex, multi-layered dynamics, allows you to release some of the guilt that you may feel. It's important to remember that sometimes, no matter how much we love or try to influence others, their decisions are theirs to make.

Finding Grace and Self-Compassion in a Painful Narrative

Perhaps the most difficult part of dealing with guilt and self-blame is finding the space to forgive yourself. It's easy to become trapped in a painful narrative of failure—especially when the estrangement feels so deeply personal. The guilt may make you feel that you were not enough, that you did something wrong, or that you should have done more. However, embracing self-compassion is essential for healing.

Self-compassion means treating yourself with the same kindness, care, and understanding that you would offer to a close friend in a similar situation. It's about acknowledging your pain and the difficulty of the situation, and being gentle with yourself in the face of those emotions. When you begin to practice self-compassion, you stop viewing yourself as the problem and instead see yourself as someone who is navigating a tough and painful situation with love and grace.

One way to cultivate self-compassion is to challenge negative self-talk. Instead of telling yourself that you are a failure, remind yourself of the times you showed love, care, and devotion to your grandchild. Remind yourself that you did your best with the information and circumstances you had at the time. Even if things didn't work out the way you had hoped, your love for your grandchild is still real and valuable.

Another key to self-compassion is learning to accept that the estrangement is not a reflection of your worth. Your grandchild's decision to distance themselves from you may be based on many factors—some of which are completely outside of your control. In time, you may come to understand that the estrangement is not a measure of your love, value, or role as a grandparent. It's simply a part of a larger, complicated family dynamic.

It's also important to recognize that self-compassion doesn't mean accepting everything that happened without question—it means recognizing that you are human, and as such, you will make mistakes and face challenges. But those mistakes do not define you. Your identity as a loving, caring grandparent remains intact, regardless of the estrangement.

Conclusion

Guilt is a powerful emotion, and when coupled with self-blame, it can be overwhelming. However, for grandparents experiencing estrangement from their grandchildren, much of this guilt is misplaced. It is essential to understand what is within your control and what is not, so that you can release the weight of unwarranted guilt and begin to heal. By cultivating grace, compassion, and forgiveness for yourself, you can begin to rewrite the painful narrative of estrangement. Remember, you did not fail. You loved with all your heart, and while you may not have been able to control the outcome, your love remains steadfast. It is through self-compassion that you will find the peace you seek, as you come to terms with the situation and heal from the pain of estrangement.

WHEN YOU'RE THE VILLAIN IN THEIR STORY

Introduction

Estrangement can often feel like a one-sided story, where your voice is silenced, and your version of events is lost in the noise of family conflict. When you become the villain in someone else's narrative—especially within your own family—the pain can feel unbearable. It's as though the very love and care you've given are twisted into something harmful or inadequate. This chapter delves into the experience of being mischaracterized within the family, especially when triangulation, distorted narratives, and rewritten histories play a role in shaping perceptions. We will explore the dynamics of family triangulation, how the children of your children may be shielded from your love, and how to cope with painful accusations and unfair characterizations that often accompany estrangement. By understanding these dynamics, you will be better equipped to navigate the emotional challenges of being portrayed as the villain in someone else's story.

Understanding Family Triangulation, Narratives, and Rewritten Histories

Family triangulation occurs when one person (often a parent or child) uses a third party—usually another family member or a relative—to communicate, influence, or manipulate a situation. In the context of estrangement, triangulation can exacerbate the rift, making it more difficult for grandparents to directly address the issue with their children or grandchildren. Triangulation often involves the spread of one-sided narratives, where the estranged grandparent becomes the scapegoat or villain, and their perspective is not given space to be heard.

Triangulation can happen subtly or overtly. A parent may subtly influence their child's perception of their grandparent by telling them about past grievances or issues, distorting the grandparent's role in the family. In some cases, triangulation is more overt—such as when a child or family member tells others directly negative stories about the grandparent, framing them as the instigator of the conflict or as someone who is untrustworthy, negligent, or unloving. Over time, this type of triangulation leads to a false narrative, where the grandparent's love and intentions are ignored or misinterpreted.

In the case of estrangement, triangulation often results in a fractured family dynamic, where one person's viewpoint is amplified at the expense of others. The estranged grandparent may find themselves falsely accused, with no opportunity to defend themselves or explain their side. It can feel like a relentless cycle, where every effort to reconnect or communicate is thwarted by these external forces. The reality, however, is often much more complex—shaped by misunderstandings, unresolved tensions, and competing interests.

As triangulation continues, the grandparent's image may be rewritten in the family's collective memory. Past incidents that were once viewed as minor misunderstandings can be reinterpreted as significant betrayals. Small conflicts become magnified, and past attempts at reconciliation are erased or dismissed. The grandparent is no longer seen as a source of love and support, but as the antagonist in a family drama that unfolds without their participation.

How Children of Your Children May Be Shielded from Your Love

One of the most heartbreaking aspects of estrangement for grandparents is the realization that their grandchildren—the children of their children—are being shielded from their love. Grandparents often hold the deepest affection for their grandchildren, feeling an overwhelming sense of pride, joy, and responsibility in watching them grow. However, when estrangement occurs, this bond is severed, and the emotional toll is felt by both the grandparent and the grandchild.

In some cases, children may be deliberately kept away from their grandparents due to the influence of the parents (the grandparent's own children). These parents may view their relationship with the grandparent as strained or broken, and out of resentment, anger, or a desire to protect their own children, they may actively block the grandparent's attempts to maintain contact. This is often an example of family triangulation at play—where the child is made to feel that the grandparent is untrustworthy or harmful, based on the parent's influence.

In such cases, the grandparent's love is not only unrecognized but actively obstructed. The child may grow up without knowing the warmth, wisdom, and unconditional love of their grandparent, and this loss can feel even more painful when the grandparent realizes that their relationship with the grandchild has been manipulated by the parents. The grandparent may never have had the opportunity to show their grandchild the love they have to offer, and the child may be deprived of an important familial connection that could have enriched their lives.

This dynamic can be particularly hurtful because it is often based on a false premise. The grandparent may have been shut out not because of any real wrongdoing but because of preconceived biases or one-sided narratives. The result is a relationship lost—one that the grandparent longs to repair but is told they cannot, because the parent has decided otherwise. This emotional exclusion often creates a sense of powerlessness in grandparents, who are left wondering how they could have been part of their grandchild's life but were prevented from doing so.

Coping with Unfair Characterizations and Painful Accusations

Being mischaracterized as the villain in a family story is not just emotionally painful—it can be deeply confusing and disorienting. When you've spent years building a relationship based on love, care, and shared experiences, only to have it rewritten in a negative light, it can feel as though your entire identity as a grandparent is being erased. The pain of this misrepresentation is compounded by the inability to set the record straight, as the estrangement itself often creates barriers to communication.

Here are a few strategies for coping with these unfair characterizations and painful accusations:

1. Acknowledge Your Pain

The first step in coping with unfair characterizations is acknowledging the pain they bring. It's important to give yourself permission to feel hurt, frustrated, and angry. These feelings are valid—after all, your love has been misunderstood, and your intentions have been questioned. Allow yourself to sit with these emotions and process them in a healthy way. Journaling, speaking to a counselor, or reaching out to a trusted friend can provide a supportive space to express your feelings.

2. Recognize That the Narrative May Not Be the Whole Truth

It's crucial to understand that when you are portrayed as the villain in someone else's story, that narrative may be incomplete or distorted. No single person's perspective captures the full reality of a situation. Family dynamics are complicated, and estrangement often results from a mix of factors, not just one individual's actions. The narrative you are being portrayed in may omit key details—your love, your efforts to maintain the relationship, and the ways in which you tried to support your family.

Try to resist internalizing the unfair characterizations. While you may not have the opportunity to correct the narrative within the family, remind yourself that the truth of your relationship with your grandchild is not defined by the opinions or accusations of others. The love you have for them remains, regardless of how the situation is framed.

3. Create Boundaries Around the Narrative

It's easy to become consumed by the narrative others are creating, especially if it directly contradicts your own version of events. However, it's essential to set emotional boundaries around these stories. Allowing yourself to engage in the negativity and unfair characterizations can lead to unnecessary emotional turmoil. While you can't control what others say or believe, you can control how much of it you internalize.

Focus on maintaining your sense of identity and self-worth, separate from the accusations and distorted stories. Practice self-care, and find ways to affirm your value as a person, not just as a grandparent. The love and care you have given, and the memories you have created, are part of who you are, and no external narrative can erase that.

4. Seek Validation Outside the Family

Estrangement can create a deep sense of isolation, but it's important to seek validation and support outside of the family. Trusted friends, therapists, or support groups can offer much-needed perspective and understanding. Sometimes, hearing from people who are not involved in the family conflict can help you see the situation more clearly and remind you that your grief is valid.

Additionally, finding a community of other grandparents who have experienced similar challenges can be empowering. You are not alone in this journey, and hearing others' stories can provide a sense of solidarity and connection. These outside sources of support can help you rebuild your emotional resilience and offer a safe space to share your feelings without fear of judgment.

5. Find Peace in Letting Go of Control

As painful as it may be, the reality of estrangement is that there is only so much you can do to change the situation. If the family narrative is beyond your control, you may need to accept that it's okay to let go of the need to change other people's perceptions. While this doesn't mean giving up on the relationship, it means recognizing that your peace of mind should not hinge on the approval or understanding of others.

By letting go of the need to defend yourself against every unfair characterization, you can focus on what is within your control—healing, finding peace, and embracing the love you still have for your grandchild, even from a distance. In time, you may find that releasing the need to change the narrative offers you the freedom to heal and move forward with hope.

Conclusion

When you are cast as the villain in someone else's family story, the emotional toll can be overwhelming. Unfair characterizations, painful accusations, and the influence of triangulation create a complex emotional landscape for estranged grandparents to navigate. However, by understanding these dynamics and learning to differentiate between what you can control and what is beyond your power, you can begin to cope with the pain of being mischaracterized. Finding peace in letting go of the need to defend yourself or correct the narrative is a crucial step toward healing. Remember, your love for your grandchild and your role as a grandparent are not defined by the stories others tell. The truth of your heart remains, even in the silence and distance.

PART III
HEALING WITHOUT CLOSURE

LOVE LETTERS THAT NEVER AGE

Introduction

In the quiet spaces left by estrangement, there's a deep yearning to connect—an ache for words left unsaid, for love that feels untouchable. For grandparents who find themselves separated from their grandchildren, the absence can feel all-encompassing. The silence between you can seem like an impenetrable wall, leaving you unsure of how to communicate the love, care, and wisdom you wish to share. Yet, there is a way to bridge that gap—through the act of writing. Love letters, though unsent, can become a powerful means of expressing the depth of your feelings, documenting your memories, and preserving your connection in a way that time and distance cannot diminish. In this chapter, we will explore how writing unsent letters can be a therapeutic outlet, a way to keep the flame of love alive in the absence of physical presence. We will also discuss how to create symbolic rituals to honor your relationship and explore the practice of memory-keeping to ensure that your love is documented, even if it cannot be fully expressed in the present.

Writing Unsent Letters to Your Grandchild

Writing letters to your grandchild, even if they will never be read, can be an incredibly healing practice. It allows you to articulate the emotions that may feel too painful to express verbally, especially if the relationship has been severed. The letters become a space where you can express everything you wish you could say but can't—whether that's love, regret, hope, or longing.

These unsent letters offer a sense of continuity in a relationship that feels broken. When words are left unspoken, they can fester inside, causing unresolved emotions to build up. Writing them down in a letter allows you to externalize your feelings, making them easier to process and understand. It's a way to let go of the internal conflict, if only for a moment, and find peace in expressing your heart.

In these letters, you can say everything you wish you had been able to say in person. You can tell your grandchild about the love you have for them, the memories you cherish, the lessons you've learned throughout your life, and the hopes you have for their future. You can talk about the things you would have done together, the experiences you would have shared, and the moments that would have made you proud. Through the process of writing, you create a symbolic space for those words to exist, even if they're not physically shared.

For some grandparents, the idea of unsent letters may seem sad, as they represent a love that cannot be fully expressed in the present moment. But it's important to understand that these letters are not just about closure or sending a message—they're about preserving your emotions and affirming your connection with your grandchild. The act of writing becomes a declaration of love, a statement that no matter the distance, your feelings remain unchanged. It is a way of saying, "I still love you. I still care. I still remember you."

You can write these letters regularly, allowing yourself to freely express whatever is in your heart at that moment. Whether you choose to keep them in a safe place for yourself, bury them in a journal, or even burn them as a symbolic release, these letters become a means of processing your grief, holding onto your love, and nurturing a sense of connection despite the physical absence.

Creating Symbolic Rituals to Honor the Relationship

When estrangement creates a void in your life, creating rituals can provide comfort and a sense of connection. Rituals help to reaffirm the bond between grandparent and grandchild, offering a way to honor the relationship despite the circumstances. These rituals do not require physical presence—they are symbolic acts that allow you to stay connected to your grandchild, even if they are not actively involved in your life.

Symbolic rituals can take many forms. For example, you might choose to celebrate special occasions like your grandchild's birthday or other milestones, even if you are not able to be present. This could involve lighting a candle in their honor, writing a letter, or simply taking a moment to reflect on the memories you've shared. By doing so, you create a way of acknowledging the significance of the relationship, even when you are physically separated.

Another powerful ritual might involve keeping an object or memento that reminds you of your grandchild—a gift they gave you, a photo from when they were younger, or a cherished keepsake. You can incorporate this object into your daily life as a way to honor the bond you still share. For example, you might display a picture of your grandchild in your home, not as a symbol of loss, but as a reminder of the love that persists beyond the estrangement. Every time you look at that picture or hold that object, you can silently affirm the connection that is still very much alive in your heart.

Another meaningful ritual might involve planting a tree or flower in your grandchild's name—an act that represents growth, life, and continuity. Each time you tend to the plant, you can remember the joy your grandchild brought into your life and continue to nurture the love you share, even if you cannot physically nurture the relationship. These symbolic gestures may not immediately heal the pain of estrangement, but they provide a gentle reminder that love doesn't disappear when people are apart. It can be sustained through ritual, memory, and meaningful action.

Memory-Keeping: How to Document Love in the Absence of Presence

Memory-keeping is another beautiful way to preserve your relationship with your grandchild in the absence of physical presence. While estrangement can feel like a form of erasure—like the love you once shared is being forgotten—memory-keeping allows you to actively preserve and celebrate the connection, even if you are not able to be part of your grandchild's life right now.

There are many ways to document love through memory-keeping. Journaling is one of the most intimate and personal ways to record your feelings and thoughts. You can write about the moments you've shared with your grandchild—whether that's trips to the park, shared meals, or quiet moments of connection. You can also document what you would have wanted to share with them if the estrangement hadn't occurred—the things you would have taught them, the wisdom you would have passed down, and the memories you would have created together.

In addition to journaling, you can create a scrapbook or photo album filled with memories. Include pictures, mementos, and notes from the times you spent with your grandchild. This is not just a way to remember the past—it's a way to keep the love alive. When you create a scrapbook, you are actively choosing to hold onto the memories that bring you joy, the experiences that shaped your relationship, and the moments that remind you of the deep connection you once shared. This book can serve as a legacy of love—a collection of memories that will remain, no matter what happens with the relationship.

Some grandparents choose to create a video diary or a letter over time, speaking to their grandchild about their life, their hopes, and their love. This is a way of documenting a relationship that may not be actively taking place in the present but continues to be a vital part of your life. Whether you share these videos or letters with your grandchild now or in the future, they become a testament to your love and devotion.

Memory-keeping allows you to embrace the love you still feel, even in the midst of estrangement. It helps to preserve the connection between you and your grandchild in a tangible way, offering a sense of comfort and continuity. Whether it's through writing, scrapbooking, or keeping special mementos, you are creating a legacy that is not defined by estrangement but by love and memory.

Conclusion

Estrangement is a painful and complex journey, but love does not easily fade. Writing unsent letters, creating symbolic rituals, and engaging in memory-keeping are powerful ways to hold onto the bond you share with your grandchild, even when physical presence is not possible. These practices offer a way to express your love, process your grief, and preserve the connection that still exists in your heart. Though the distance may feel vast, these acts of remembrance create a bridge—a way to honor the love that has not disappeared, even in the absence of physical contact. Remember, your love for your grandchild is timeless, and through these rituals, letters, and memories, you ensure that your connection endures, no matter the distance.

CHAPTER 8

MAKING PEACE WITH THE NOT-KNOWING

Introduction

One of the most difficult aspects of estrangement is the uncertainty. The unknown—whether the relationship with your grandchild will ever be repaired, whether you will ever have the chance to speak again, or whether things will ever go back to how they once were—can weigh heavily on your heart. It's a kind of grief that doesn't have a clear resolution or endpoint. There is no defined "closure," no promise of reconciliation, and no way of knowing what the future holds. This chapter explores how to live with the not-knowing. We will discuss how to make peace with the uncertainty of estrangement, how to let go without giving up hope, and how mindfulness techniques can help you cope with the anxiety and sorrow that often accompany this emotional journey. By accepting that not everything can be controlled or predicted, you can find a deeper sense of peace within yourself, regardless of the outcome of the estrangement.

Living with the Uncertainty of Possible Reconnection

When estrangement occurs, it often feels like the door to the relationship has been shut, with no clear indication of when—or if—it will ever be opened again. For many grandparents, the hope of reconnection is always present, flickering in the background. The possibility of repairing the bond with their grandchild remains a distant but real desire. However, the uncertainty surrounding this hope can be both comforting and painful.

The unknown nature of estrangement can leave you stuck in a place of "waiting"—waiting for a phone call, an apology, an acknowledgment. It's easy to become consumed by this waiting, fixating on the possibility of reconnection, and yet never knowing when or if it will happen. It's a kind of limbo that can be difficult to escape. You may spend hours wondering what your grandchild is doing, whether they miss you, or if they are even thinking about you. It's a natural reaction to the situation, and it comes from a deep love and longing to reconnect.

However, the reality is that you cannot control when or if the estrangement will end. While hope is important, living in constant anticipation of a possible reconnection can prevent you from fully embracing the present moment. The uncertainty of estrangement can cause emotional strain, as you find yourself oscillating between hope and despair, waiting for something that may or may not happen. It can feel like you're stuck between the past and the future, unable to truly live in the present.

Making peace with the not-knowing involves acknowledging the possibility of reconnection without letting it define your emotional state. It means holding space for hope while also allowing yourself to move forward, regardless of the outcome. This may seem counterintuitive—how can you let go of something you long for? But by accepting that the future is uncertain, you free yourself from the emotional weight of constantly waiting for a resolution. Instead, you can focus on what you can control—your emotional well-being, your personal growth, and how you respond to the estrangement.

One of the most empowering things you can do is to stop placing all of your emotional energy into the possibility of reconciliation. Instead, shift your focus to the present. Take stock of what you have now—your memories, your resilience, your ability to love—and allow those things to provide comfort in the absence of certainty. By living in the present moment, you can reduce the power of uncertainty and learn to accept it as part of the natural ebb and flow of life.

Letting Go Without Giving Up

Letting go is often viewed as an act of surrender—a giving up, a giving in, or a sign of defeat. When it comes to estrangement, the idea of "letting go" can feel like you're abandoning hope, giving up on the possibility of ever reconnecting with your grandchild. But letting go in this context is not about giving up; it's about releasing the emotional grip that the situation has on you. It's about finding peace with what is, rather than constantly longing for what could be.

Letting go means accepting that, while you may still love your grandchild, the estrangement is a reality that you cannot change on your own. You cannot force reconciliation, and you cannot control the actions of others. Letting go is about freeing yourself from the emotional burden of trying to control an outcome that is beyond your power. It's about acknowledging that the estrangement, whether temporary or permanent, is a part of the larger story, but it does not define your entire relationship with your grandchild.

Letting go also involves releasing the guilt and self-blame that often accompany estrangement. It's about recognizing that you are not solely responsible for the rupture, and that sometimes, no matter how much love and effort you give, things are out of your control. This doesn't mean you stop caring or that you stop hoping for reconciliation. It means you stop carrying the weight of responsibility and you stop allowing the estrangement to dictate your happiness or sense of peace.

By letting go, you create space for yourself to heal and to live fully in the present. You may still hope for reconnection, but you no longer depend on it as your source of emotional fulfillment. You understand that your life is rich and meaningful, regardless of the status of the estrangement. Letting go is not about losing love; it's about shifting your emotional focus and finding a new way of relating to the situation. It's about giving yourself the grace to move forward, even if you don't have all the answers.

Mindfulness Techniques for Anxiety and Sorrow

Estrangement can bring with it a great deal of anxiety and sorrow. The uncertainty of whether the relationship will ever be repaired can lead to constant worry, and the emotional pain of separation can feel overwhelming. Mindfulness practices can be a powerful tool for managing the anxiety and sorrow that come with estrangement. Mindfulness encourages you to be present in the moment, without judgment, and to accept your feelings without trying to suppress them.

Here are some mindfulness techniques that can help you cope with the emotional weight of estrangement:

1. Breathing Exercises

Breathing exercises are one of the simplest and most effective ways to calm your mind and reduce anxiety. When you find yourself overwhelmed by worry or sorrow, take a few moments to focus on your breath. Inhale deeply through your nose, hold for a few seconds, and then exhale slowly through your mouth. This simple act can help ground you in the present moment and bring a sense of calm to your body and mind.

You can also practice deep breathing with a focus on releasing tension. As you breathe in, imagine drawing in peace and love. As you breathe out, imagine releasing the pain, frustration, or anxiety that you may be holding. This technique helps to create a sense of emotional release and helps to regulate your nervous system.

2. Body Scan Meditation

A body scan meditation is a mindfulness practice where you bring your attention to different parts of your body, noticing any areas of tension or discomfort, and consciously relaxing them. This practice helps you become more attuned to your body's physical sensations and can help release pent-up emotional stress.

Start by lying down in a quiet space, or sitting comfortably with your feet flat on the floor. Close your eyes and begin by focusing on your toes, noticing any sensations of tension or discomfort. Slowly work your way up your body, scanning each part and allowing it to relax. As you reach your chest, heart, and mind, acknowledge any emotions you are carrying, and allow them to be present without judgment. This practice can help release emotional tension and bring you into a place of acceptance.

3. Loving-Kindness Meditation

Loving-kindness meditation is a practice where you focus on sending love and compassion to yourself and others. This meditation can be particularly helpful when you feel the emotional weight of estrangement. By practicing loving-kindness, you cultivate compassion, not only for others but also for yourself.

To practice, sit comfortably and close your eyes. Begin by directing loving-kindness toward yourself, repeating the phrases: "May I be happy. May I be healthy. May I be at peace." Then, gradually expand this love to others in your life. First, send love to your grandchild, even if you are estranged, with the phrases: "May you be happy. May you be healthy. May you be at peace." Continue by sending love to other family members or even strangers. This practice helps foster a sense of peace and emotional connection, despite the distance.

4. Mindful Journaling

Mindful journaling involves writing down your thoughts and feelings without judgment, allowing you to express your emotions freely. This technique helps you process anxiety and sorrow by putting your feelings into words. It can be particularly useful when dealing with the uncertainty of estrangement. Start by writing whatever is on your mind, without trying to edit or censor yourself. Let your thoughts flow freely onto the page.

After writing, reflect on how the practice made you feel. Did it bring relief? Did it help you release some of the emotional weight you were carrying? Mindful journaling helps you process and release negative emotions, bringing clarity and peace to your emotional landscape.

Conclusion

Living with the uncertainty of estrangement is one of the most challenging emotional experiences a grandparent can face. The not-knowing about the possibility of reconnection can feel consuming, and the sorrow of separation can seem endless. However, by embracing the uncertainty, letting go without giving up, and using mindfulness techniques, you can find a sense of peace. Mindfulness helps you remain grounded in the present moment, reducing anxiety and allowing space for healing. While the estrangement may never have a clear resolution, making peace with the not-knowing allows you to live fully and move forward with grace. Your love for your grandchild remains, and by accepting the uncertainty, you make room for personal growth, emotional peace, and the hope that, no matter the outcome, your heart will continue to heal.

CHAPTER 9

THE GRANDPARENT'S GRIEF CIRCLE – YOU ARE NOT ALONE

Introduction

Estrangement from grandchildren is a heart-wrenching and isolating experience, one that often leaves grandparents feeling like they are navigating an emotional wilderness. Unlike the grief associated with death, estrangement carries with it an ambiguous and complex emotional burden—there is no closure, no finality, and often no space in society to mourn the loss of a relationship that is still technically alive. As a result, estranged grandparents often find themselves carrying their grief in silence, without the support or understanding that might be offered in other circumstances.

But this grief is not unique to you. It's a silent epidemic that many grandparents face, often in isolation. However, you are not alone on this journey. There are others who understand the unique pain of estrangement—others who have walked the same path, struggled with the same emotions, and yearned for the same reconciliation. This chapter aims to shine a light on the shared experience of estranged grandparents, offering validation, insight, and resources to help you feel connected to a larger community of support. Through personal stories, support groups, online communities, and therapy, you can find comfort, guidance, and companionship as you navigate your own grief journey.

The Silent Epidemic of Estranged Grandparents

The grief of estranged grandparents is often a silent one. Unlike the grief that follows the death of a loved one, which is widely acknowledged and supported by society, estrangement grief is often dismissed or minimized. Grandparents may feel as though their pain is not valid because the person they are grieving is still alive, even if the relationship is cut off. This can make estranged grandparents feel invisible, as though their grief is not recognized or understood by others.

Unfortunately, the numbers of estranged grandparents are growing. According to studies, a significant percentage of grandparents report experiencing estrangement from their grandchildren, often due to divorce, family conflict, or parental alienation. This issue is more widespread than many realize, and yet it remains largely unspoken. There are no public mourning rituals for estranged grandparents, no recognition of their pain within the community. As a result, grandparents often suffer in silence, feeling isolated and alone in their grief.

Estranged grandparents may also experience feelings of shame, as if they are somehow at fault for the estrangement. This can make it even harder to reach out for support, as they may fear being judged or misunderstood. The lack of societal acknowledgment for this form of grief only exacerbates the emotional burden, leading many grandparents to internalize their pain rather than seek help.

Stories from Others on the Same Journey

One of the most powerful ways to understand that you are not alone in your experience is to hear the stories of others who have walked a similar path. The emotional journey of estranged grandparents is one that is marked by shared themes—feelings of loss, guilt, confusion, and longing—but each individual story is unique. Listening to the experiences of others can help you feel seen and heard, and it can offer comfort in knowing that there are others who truly understand what you're going through.

Take, for example, the story of Margaret, a grandmother who has not seen her grandchildren in over three years. She recounts how, at first, she felt completely blindsided by the estrangement. "I thought I was doing everything right," she says. "I was supportive, I respected boundaries, and I loved my grandkids with all my heart. But one day, it all changed. The silence started, and I didn't know why. It was like I disappeared from their lives without warning. And no one would tell me why."

Margaret's story is not unique. Many grandparents experience the sudden onset of estrangement, often without a clear explanation or warning. The pain of not knowing why the relationship was severed, combined with the helplessness of not being able to change the situation, can feel overwhelming.

Then there's Tom, a grandfather who has experienced estrangement due to a contentious divorce between his son and daughter-in-law. "It's like I'm being punished for something I didn't do," he explains. "I've always tried to be supportive, but my son's ex-wife doesn't want me to have any contact with the kids. I understand that they've been through a lot, but it doesn't seem fair. My grandchildren deserve to know me."

Tom's feelings of injustice are shared by many grandparents who find themselves at the mercy of family dynamics that are out of their control. Whether it's a divorce, a falling out between parents, or a breakdown in communication, estranged grandparents often feel that they are being unjustly kept from their grandchildren.

Both Margaret and Tom's stories, like countless others, reflect the deep pain that estranged grandparents experience. But they also reflect resilience—the ability to keep going, to keep loving, and to keep hoping, even in the face of seemingly insurmountable obstacles. Their stories are a reminder that, even in the midst of heartbreak, there is strength in community, in shared experiences, and in the simple act of knowing that others have walked the same difficult road.

How Support Groups, Online Communities, and Therapy Help

Finding support is one of the most important steps in healing from estrangement grief. The pain of being cut off from your grandchild can feel unbearable, but when you find others who understand your experience, the burden becomes lighter. Support groups, online communities, and therapy can provide a vital space for grandparents to share their feelings, receive validation, and gain insights into how to cope with their grief.

1. Support Groups

Support groups for estranged grandparents provide a safe space where individuals can share their experiences, express their emotions, and offer advice to others who are going through similar struggles. These groups can be found locally or online, and they are often led by professionals who understand the complexities of estrangement and grief.

Being part of a support group can help you realize that you are not alone in your experience. Hearing from others who have faced the same challenges can provide comfort and a sense of solidarity. It can also give you a sense of perspective, helping you see that while estrangement is painful, it is not an isolated experience—it is part of a larger, shared narrative of loss and healing.

Support groups also offer practical tools and strategies for coping with the emotional weight of estrangement. Whether it's advice on how to reach out to your grandchild, tips on managing the emotional ups and downs of the journey, or simply a space to vent your frustration and sadness, these groups provide a sense of connection and support that is invaluable in the healing process.

2. Online Communities

For many estranged grandparents, online communities can be an essential source of support. These communities provide a virtual space where grandparents from all over the world can connect, share their stories, and offer advice. Online forums and social media groups dedicated to estranged grandparents have become an increasingly popular way for people to find community and support, especially when in-person support groups may not be available.

The advantage of online communities is that they offer anonymity and the ability to connect with people who may have similar experiences but are geographically distant. They also provide a sense of continuity, as grandparents can log on at any time to share their feelings, ask for advice, or simply read the experiences of others. Many online communities have become a lifeline for those who feel isolated or who don't have anyone in their immediate circle who understands their pain.

3. Therapy

Therapy can also be a valuable tool in navigating the emotional challenges of estrangement. A licensed therapist who specializes in family dynamics or grief can provide personalized guidance and help you work through the complex emotions that come with estrangement. Therapy can offer a safe space to process your feelings of sadness, guilt, and frustration, and it can help you develop coping strategies for managing these emotions.

One of the key benefits of therapy is the ability to examine the estrangement from an objective perspective. A therapist can help you understand the broader family dynamics at play, which can often reduce feelings of self-blame and offer new insights into the situation. Therapy can also help you process the grief of estrangement and develop strategies for coping with the uncertainty of possible reconciliation.

Conclusion

Estrangement grief can be an isolating and painful experience, but it doesn't have to be faced alone. The silent epidemic of estranged grandparents is far more common than many realize, and there are supportive communities, groups, and professionals who can offer guidance, understanding, and connection. Through sharing stories with others who have walked the same path, finding support in online communities, and seeking professional therapy, you can begin to navigate the emotional complexities of estrangement. The journey of estrangement may not have a clear resolution, but by reaching out for support, you can ease the burden, find solace, and move toward healing. You are not alone in this journey, and with the right support, you can find hope, healing, and peace, even amidst the pain.

PART IV
FINDING HOPE IN THE HEARTACHE

CHAPTER 10

HOLDING ON, LETTING GO – A NEW RELATIONSHIP WITH HOPE

Introduction

Hope is a powerful force. It can guide us through the darkest of times, inspire us to keep moving forward, and provide a sense of meaning when the path seems uncertain. For grandparents who have experienced estrangement from their grandchildren, hope often plays a complex and ambivalent role. It can be a source of strength, but it can also fuel a cycle of endless waiting, leaving you stuck in a place of uncertainty and longing. In this chapter, we will explore how to reframe hope—not as a continuous yearning for reunion, but as a source of inner peace and quiet strength. We will discuss how to move from waiting for reconciliation to embracing hope in a way that allows you to reclaim your time, identity, and joy. Through this process of holding on and letting go, you can cultivate a new relationship with hope—one that brings you peace, no matter the outcome of the estrangement.

Reframing Hope: From Reunion to Inner Peace

Hope is often seen as the expectation of something better in the future—perhaps a reunion with a grandchild, a chance for healing, or the restoration of a broken relationship. For many grandparents who are estranged, this type of hope can feel all-consuming. It's easy to believe that everything will be okay if the relationship is repaired. Yet, this kind of hope can also keep you emotionally tethered to the past, perpetuating a sense of waiting for something that may or may not happen.

Reframing hope is about shifting your focus from the external outcome—a reunion or reconciliation—to a more internal sense of peace. It is about accepting that while the possibility of reconnection exists, it is not the sole source of your happiness or fulfillment. Rather than waiting for someone else's actions or decisions to bring you peace, you begin to find peace within yourself. This doesn't mean giving up on reconciliation; it simply means allowing hope to evolve from a future-focused desire into a present-focused feeling of inner calm.

To begin reframing hope, it helps to consider the following shift in perspective:

1. **Hope as Acceptance** – Instead of clinging to a specific future outcome, hope becomes the ability to accept the situation as it is right now. This doesn't mean giving up on the possibility of change, but rather accepting that the future is unknown and that peace is available in the present moment. You can hope for a better relationship with your grandchild while also accepting that this relationship may never return to what it once was.

2. **Hope as Empowerment** – Hope shifts from a passive waiting game to an active force that empowers you to live your life in the present. It becomes the belief that you can create meaning and joy regardless of the estrangement. This kind of hope doesn't depend on the actions of others but is rooted in your ability to navigate life with resilience and grace.

3. **Hope as Gratitude** – Reframing hope also means finding gratitude in what you have right now. It's the practice of focusing on what is still intact, what you still cherish, and what you still have control over in your life. Even if the relationship with your grandchild is strained, you can still find hope in the memories you shared, in the love you have for them, and in your ability to carry that love forward.

By reframing hope, you can begin to cultivate an inner peace that doesn't depend on external circumstances. You may not have control over the estrangement, but you do have control over how you respond to it. This kind of hope is liberating—it allows you to live fully, regardless of whether or not the relationship is repaired.

Hope as Quiet Strength vs. Endless Waiting

When hope is tied solely to a future reunion or resolution, it can often lead to a cycle of endless waiting. You find yourself constantly holding out for the moment when your grandchild will return to your life, when the silence will be broken, or when the estrangement will be lifted. This kind of hope can be exhausting, as it leaves you in a state of emotional limbo, waiting for something outside of yourself to change in order for you to feel at peace.

In contrast, hope as quiet strength is rooted in the understanding that while you can't control the future, you can control how you approach the present. It's the ability to remain hopeful without relying on a specific outcome. This hope is steady, resilient, and anchored in the belief that your life is still valuable and meaningful, even in the midst of estrangement.

Hope as quiet strength is the strength to move forward with purpose, even when you don't have all the answers. It's about finding peace in the process of life itself, rather than waiting for a specific resolution to bring you happiness. When hope shifts in this way, it allows you to focus on what you can influence—your own well-being, your relationships with others, and your ability to continue growing and healing, regardless of what happens with your grandchild.

The key difference between hope as quiet strength and endless waiting is agency. Endless waiting often feels like a passive experience—an emotional holding pattern where you wait for someone else's actions to determine your next step. Hope as quiet strength, on the other hand, involves taking proactive steps to live your life fully. It's about letting go of the need for things to be a certain way in order to feel whole and embracing the freedom that comes with knowing you can move forward, no matter the uncertainty.

Reclaiming Your Time, Identity, and Joy

Estrangement can often rob you of your sense of identity, especially when being a grandparent was such an integral part of your life. The absence of your grandchild's presence can make you question your role in the family, your worth as a grandparent, and the meaning of your life moving forward. It's easy to become defined by the estrangement, to feel like it is the central story of your life. But reclaiming your time, identity, and joy is an important step in healing and moving forward.

1. Reclaiming Your Time

Estrangement can consume your thoughts and emotions, making it difficult to focus on anything else. You may find yourself waiting for a phone call, checking for messages, or wondering when the silence will end. However, reclaiming your time means rediscovering what brings you joy, purpose, and fulfillment outside of the estrangement.

Consider how you can fill your time with activities that nourish your soul—whether it's spending time with other family members, pursuing a hobby you love, volunteering, or dedicating time to self-care. The more you reclaim your time and focus on activities that bring you fulfillment, the more you can begin to free yourself from the emotional hold that the estrangement has over your life.

2. Reclaiming Your Identity

Your identity as a grandparent is an important part of who you are, but it is not the only part. When estrangement occurs, it can feel like you've lost a significant piece of yourself. But reclaiming your identity involves recognizing that while your role as a grandparent is important, you are also an individual with your own passions, talents, and worth.

Take time to reconnect with who you are outside of the estranged relationship. Reflect on what brings you joy, what goals you still want to achieve, and what legacy you want to leave. By focusing on your own growth and development, you can reclaim a sense of self that is not defined solely by the estrangement but is instead rooted in your own strengths and desires.

3. Reclaiming Your Joy

Joy is a powerful antidote to the sorrow of estrangement. While it may feel difficult to experience joy in the midst of pain, reclaiming your joy is essential for healing. This doesn't mean forgetting about the estrangement or pretending that it doesn't hurt, but rather making room for moments of happiness, laughter, and contentment, even in the face of hardship.

Reclaim your joy by engaging in activities that uplift you—whether it's spending time with friends, enjoying nature, practicing mindfulness, or simply doing something that makes you smile. Joy is not an indication that you are "over" the estrangement; rather, it is a sign that you are embracing life in its fullness, despite the pain. Reclaiming your joy is about finding balance and rediscovering what makes life worth living, even when things are uncertain.

Conclusion

Hope, when reframed, becomes a source of inner peace rather than endless waiting. It shifts from an expectation of a specific future outcome to a quiet strength that empowers you to live fully in the present. By letting go of the need for reconciliation in order to feel complete, you can begin to reclaim your time, identity, and joy. Estrangement does not define your worth or your ability to love—it simply represents a chapter in the broader story of your life. Holding on to hope while letting go of the need for a specific outcome allows you to move forward with strength, purpose, and peace, knowing that no matter what happens with your grandchild, you have the power to live a meaningful and fulfilling life.

THE RIPPLE OF KINDNESS – LOVING OTHER CHILDREN IN YOUR LIFE

Introduction

Estrangement from a grandchild can leave a hole in your heart—a void that no amount of reasoning or self-compassion can entirely fill. The love that you once gave so freely to your grandchild now has nowhere to go, and the absence of that relationship can leave you with a sense of loss, longing, and, often, confusion. However, even in the face of estrangement, there are still many ways to express love and care for the younger generation. In this chapter, we explore how to channel your love outward by becoming a mentor, surrogate grandparent, or community elder to other children in your life. We will discuss how to love and nurture other children—whether they are nieces, nephews, or even children of friends and neighbors—without draining your emotional reserves. By finding ways to give from the same well of love, you can heal, find new meaning, and create positive ripples in the lives of others.

Becoming a Mentor, Surrogate Grandparent, or Community Elder

While the relationship with your estranged grandchild may be painful and uncertain, it doesn't mean that your love has to be kept within a closed circle. There are many children in your life who could benefit from the wisdom, support, and care that you have to offer. Becoming a https://amazon.com/mentor, surrogate grandparent, or community elder is a way to redirect your energy into nurturing relationships that can bring both you and the children involved a sense of fulfillment, healing, and connection.

1. Mentorship

Mentoring is one of the most rewarding ways to pour love and wisdom into the life of a young person. Whether it's guiding a young student, offering career advice, or simply being a sounding board for a teenager navigating difficult life decisions, mentorship allows you to make a meaningful impact in the life of a child or young adult. You don't need to be a biological grandparent to be a mentor; many children look to other adults in their community for guidance, perspective, and encouragement.

Mentorship is an act of giving that requires patience, empathy, and listening. In becoming a mentor, you can share the experiences, values, and life lessons you've learned, helping a young person find their path. This relationship can be incredibly fulfilling, as it gives you the opportunity to connect with someone else on a deep and meaningful level while offering them the guidance and support they need.

2. Surrogate Grandparent

If the absence of a relationship with your grandchild has created a deep longing for grandparenting, consider embracing the role of a surrogate grandparent to children in your community. Surrogate grandparents are non-biological adults who offer the love, care, and wisdom that traditional grandparents might provide. These children could be the children of friends, neighbors, or even those in your extended family who are in need of emotional support and guidance.

By taking on the role of a surrogate grandparent, you can offer love, encouragement, and attention to children who might not have the presence of a grandparent in their lives. This relationship allows you to provide emotional nourishment, offer life lessons, and even engage in fun and nurturing activities, such as baking, gardening, storytelling, or simply being a comforting presence during difficult times. Being a surrogate grandparent provides an outlet for your love and caregiving instincts, allowing you to fill a void without replacing the unique bond you have with your estranged grandchild.

3. Community Elder

In addition to mentoring and grandparenting, you can also step into the role of a community elder. Elders in many cultures hold a revered position—they are seen as a source of wisdom, strength, and stability for younger generations. As a community elder, you can offer support to children who may be facing challenges, whether in the form of offering advice, hosting community events, or being a steady, loving presence that children can rely on.

Being a community elder is not about taking the place of a parent or grandparent, but rather offering a sense of consistency and emotional security for children who need it. You can provide guidance on everything from personal growth and education to life challenges and conflict resolution. This role allows you to make a lasting impact on the lives of young people in your community, and it helps you reconnect with a sense of purpose, love, and belonging.

Loving Outward When Your Own Love Is Blocked

One of the most difficult aspects of estrangement is the sense that your love has nowhere to go. When the relationship with your grandchild is blocked, it's easy to feel as though your capacity to love is being stifled. This emotional frustration can lead to feelings of sadness, anger, and helplessness. However, channeling your love outward, towards other children in your life, is one of the most powerful ways to heal from estrangement.

Loving outward involves turning your attention away from the blocked relationship and focusing on the children who are still present in your life. This act of loving others—whether through mentoring, surrogate grandparenting, or being a community elder—helps to redirect your emotional energy into something productive and fulfilling. When your own love is blocked, sharing that love with others creates a ripple effect that not only benefits the children you nurture but also brings you healing and fulfillment. It provides a sense of purpose and connection that can help mitigate the emotional pain of estrangement.

In addition to benefiting others, loving outward also helps you heal. It allows you to take the focus off of your own pain and use your experiences to empower and encourage others. This shift in perspective is powerful—it enables you to see that even in the face of loss, you can continue to give, nurture, and create positive relationships that make a real difference in the lives of those around you.

Giving from the Same Well Without Draining Yourself

While loving outward is a beautiful and healing practice, it's important to recognize that love cannot be freely given without self-care. Grandparents who are estranged may feel emotionally drained, especially if the estrangement is ongoing. The fear of being rejected, the pain of not knowing why the relationship has broken down, and the longing for reconnection can leave you feeling emotionally exhausted.

To give love to others without depleting yourself, you must first take care of your own emotional well-being. This means finding time to process your grief, setting boundaries where needed, and ensuring that you are receiving the love and care you deserve as well. Self-compassion is key—by being kind and patient with yourself, you can avoid emotional burnout and continue to give from a place of strength.

Incorporating self-care practices into your routine can help restore your energy and make it easier to love others. Whether it's through therapy, meditation, journaling, physical exercise, or simply spending time with people who uplift you, taking care of your own emotional needs ensures that you have the emotional resources to love others without sacrificing your own well-being.

It's also important to recognize that you don't have to give all of your energy at once. Love is not a finite resource; it replenishes as long as you allow yourself to rest and recharge. By setting healthy boundaries, practicing self-care, and giving love at your own pace, you can share your care with others without draining your emotional reserves.

Conclusion

Estrangement may feel like a loss of love, but it is also an invitation to share that love in new and fulfilling ways. Whether through mentoring, surrogate grandparenting, or becoming a community elder, you can channel the love you have for your grandchild into positive, nurturing relationships with other children in your life. Loving outward when your own love is blocked allows you to find healing, reclaim your sense of purpose, and make a meaningful impact in the lives of others. By giving from the same well without draining yourself, you ensure that you continue to nurture your own emotional well-being while providing love and care to those who need it most. In doing so, you not only heal your own heart but also create a ripple of kindness that extends far beyond the confines of estrangement.

BRIDGING POSSIBILITIES – IF THEY COME BACK

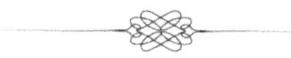

Introduction

The possibility of reconnection after estrangement is both a glimmer of hope and a source of uncertainty. For grandparents who have been separated from their grandchildren, the idea that one day, they might return—physically, emotionally, or relationally—can stir up a mixture of excitement, anxiety, and trepidation. What would it be like if they came back? What should you do if the estranged relationship begins to heal, or if your grandchild reaches out to you after a long absence?

This chapter delves into how to navigate the potential of future reconnection. Whether you're faced with a fragile beginning after a long estrangement or preparing yourself emotionally for a second chance, understanding the dynamics of this situation is key. Rebuilding a relationship that has been broken is delicate work, and being prepared—emotionally, mentally, and practically—will help you approach the situation with care, patience, and a heart open to the possibility of healing.

What to Do in Case of Future Reconnection

When estrangement ends and the possibility of reconciliation arises, it can feel like a delicate moment—one that requires thoughtful, measured action. If your grandchild reaches out to you after a long period of absence, there will likely be a rush of emotions. You might feel overjoyed and hopeful, but you might also feel cautious or unsure of how to proceed. This is a moment where the impulse to "fix everything" should be balanced with the need to approach the situation with care and mindfulness.

Here are a few steps to consider if a future reconnection occurs:

1. Stay Calm and Grounded

The first step is to remain calm. After a long estrangement, emotions will inevitably run high. Whether your grandchild contacts you through a letter, a phone call, or in person, try to stay grounded. It's easy to get swept up in the excitement or the nervousness of the moment, but remaining calm allows you to respond with clarity and grace. Take a few deep breaths, give yourself time to process the emotions that arise, and resist the urge to rush into the conversation or situation.

2. Assess the Situation Before Responding

Before jumping into the emotional exchange, take a moment to assess the situation. Consider why your grandchild has reached out, what has changed since the estrangement, and what the current circumstances are. Do you have the necessary emotional resources to engage in a meaningful, constructive conversation? Are you both ready to engage in a healthy and healing way, or is it better to take things slowly? This initial assessment is important in understanding how to proceed with the reconnection.

3. Set Boundaries and Expectations

If your grandchild reaches out, it's essential to establish boundaries and expectations—both for your own emotional well-being and for the sake of the relationship. Rebuilding a relationship after estrangement requires patience and mutual respect. You may need to communicate what you are comfortable with, whether it's the pace of communication, the level of emotional engagement, or the topics you're willing to discuss initially.

Remember, boundaries aren't about creating distance—they're about protecting yourself and the relationship as it grows. If you have concerns about emotional triggers or past unresolved issues, it's okay to express those concerns in a compassionate way. Reconnection can only be successful if both parties feel safe and respected.

4. Be Open to Their Experience

As your grandchild reaches out, it's crucial to listen to their side of the story. Their experience during the estrangement may be vastly different from your own, and it's important to approach the conversation with an open mind. Avoid the urge to defend yourself immediately or explain your actions. Instead, listen actively and empathetically. Acknowledge their feelings and experiences, even if they differ from your own. This kind of listening is vital for rebuilding trust and understanding.

5. Give It Time

Reconnection doesn't happen overnight. Even if your grandchild is reaching out with good intentions, the process of rebuilding a relationship is gradual. Be prepared for some awkwardness or hesitance at first. There may be emotional walls to break down, trust to rebuild, and misunderstandings to resolve. Be patient with the process and allow time for the relationship to unfold naturally. Sometimes, it's about taking small, consistent steps—like sharing a meal, enjoying a simple activity together, or engaging in lighthearted conversation—before diving into deeper, more emotional topics.

How to Handle Fragile Beginnings After a Long Absence

When a relationship has been estranged for an extended period, any attempt at reconciliation can feel fragile, like walking on eggshells. The emotional distance between you and your grandchild may be significant, and the wounds from the past may still be raw. If the reconnection is recent, it's important to approach it with care and sensitivity. Here are a few strategies to navigate the fragile beginnings of this new chapter:

1. Start Small and Light

In the early stages of reconnection, it's important to start small. Avoid rushing into deep or heavy topics. Instead, focus on rebuilding the foundation of the relationship with simple, neutral interactions. Ask them about their interests, hobbies, or current life events. This can help ease the tension and begin to rebuild trust gradually. Small, positive interactions will allow you to reconnect without overwhelming either party with past emotions or unresolved issues.

2. Be Patient with Emotional Responses

Estranged relationships are often filled with complex emotions—feelings of hurt, anger, confusion, and resentment may still be lingering. It's important to be patient with emotional responses, both yours and theirs. You may feel a mix of joy and fear, while your grandchild may have similar conflicting emotions. Give each other the space to express these feelings, without judgment or pressure. It's natural for emotions to surface during a reunion, but giving time for healing is crucial to the relationship's success.

3. Recognize and Respect Their Boundaries

Your grandchild may have their own boundaries and emotional needs that are important to respect. It's possible that they want to take things slowly or may not be ready to discuss the past immediately. Make sure you check in with them periodically to understand how they feel about the pace of your reconnection. Respecting their boundaries will help foster a sense of security and trust, which is essential for a successful and lasting relationship.

4. Acknowledge the Past, but Don't Dwell on It

While it's important to acknowledge the past, it's equally important not to dwell on it. You may want to discuss the reasons for the estrangement, but it's crucial not to overwhelm your grandchild with a flood of questions or accusations. Be prepared to forgive, to let go of past grievances, and to focus on moving forward. Dwelling on the past can prevent you from building a new relationship; instead, focus on understanding, healing, and creating new memories together.

Preparing Emotionally for a Second Chance – Or Not

It's important to emotionally prepare yourself for the possibility of a second chance with your grandchild, but also to prepare for the possibility that reconciliation may not happen or may take much longer than you expect. The emotional ups and downs of estrangement can make you feel vulnerable, and while hope is essential, you must also be prepared for the reality that reconciliation may not unfold as you hope.

1. Prepare for a Slow Journey

Even if your grandchild reaches out, the road to full reconciliation is rarely fast. Prepare yourself for a slow and ongoing process. There may be setbacks, awkwardness, or moments when you question whether the relationship will ever feel "normal" again. This is part of the healing journey. Patience is key, and you must be prepared to give the relationship time to develop, no matter how long it takes.

2. Guard Your Heart

Reconnecting with your grandchild is a beautiful possibility, but it's also emotionally risky. There's always the chance that things may not go as planned. It's important to guard your heart by maintaining a sense of emotional resilience. While you open yourself up to love and connection, remember that your sense of self-worth and emotional well-being should not hinge solely on the success of this reconnection. Your life is rich with meaning, regardless of the outcome of the relationship.

3. Focus on Your Healing, Regardless of the Outcome

Whether reconciliation happens or not, your own healing is paramount. Focus on nurturing your emotional well-being and growth, independent of the estranged relationship. By investing in your own mental and emotional health, you are giving yourself the best chance to approach the relationship with clarity, peace, and acceptance. If the reunion is successful, you'll be able to navigate it with a strong foundation of self-love. If reconciliation doesn't happen, you will still have the tools to maintain peace within yourself and keep moving forward.

Conclusion

The possibility of reconciliation after estrangement offers a sense of hope, but it also requires emotional preparation. The journey of reconnecting with a grandchild is delicate, and it's important to approach it with patience, open-heartedness, and respect for the past and present. While the outcome of this journey remains uncertain, you can be prepared by focusing on emotional resilience, healing, and the importance of nurturing the connection, no matter how fragile. A second chance is not just about rebuilding a relationship—it's about reclaiming peace, embracing hope, and knowing that whatever happens, you have the strength to navigate this new chapter with love and grace.

CHAPTER 13

THE GRANDCHILD I HOLD IN MY HEART

Introduction

Throughout this journey of estrangement, there has been a constant, unspoken truth: the love you have for your grandchild is unbreakable. Despite the absence, despite the distance, the bond that once existed remains a powerful part of who you are. It is a love that cannot be erased, no matter the circumstances. In this final chapter, we offer a closing letter or blessing to your grandchild—an expression of love that transcends time and space. This symbolic and healing act reinforces that your love, even from afar, is still real and sacred. You are still a grandparent, with all the joy, wisdom, and legacy that entails, regardless of the estrangement. This chapter is an opportunity to say what may have been left unsaid, to affirm your love, and to release your hopes and blessings for the future.

A Closing Letter or Blessing to the Grandchild

Dearest [Grandchild's Name],

Though we have not spoken in a long while, and though there may be silence between us, my love for you remains as strong and steadfast as it ever was. It is a love that has not diminished with time or distance, a love that exists in every corner of my heart, waiting for the moment when we might once again cross paths.

I hold you in my heart, always. In the quiet moments when the world slows down, I think of you—of the joy you brought to my life, of your laughter, your curiosity, and the ways in which you filled our time together with light. I remember the way you would run to me, the way your face lit up when we shared stories, or when we simply spent time together. These memories are treasures that I carry with me, a part of me that no amount of time or silence can take away.

I know that life can be complicated, and sometimes the paths we walk lead us in directions we never anticipated. I do not know the reasons for the distance between us, but I do know that I never stopped loving you. That love is not bound by physical presence or by the walls that may have come between us. It remains with you, wherever you are, always.

If you ever find your way back to me, know that I will be here, ready to welcome you with open arms and an open heart. And if our paths never cross again, please know that I will continue to carry you with me in spirit, holding onto the love we once shared.

I want you to know that you are always in my thoughts and prayers. I hope that life has been kind to you, that you have found joy, love, and peace along the way. I hope you've grown into the wonderful person I always knew you could be. My love for you is unconditional and everlasting, and that love is never dependent on the present moment, the misunderstandings, or the silence. It is as real as the air we breathe, and it will remain with you always.

And so, my dear [Grandchild's Name], this is my blessing to you:

May you always know the strength of love, even when it feels distant or lost. May your heart be open to forgiveness, to healing, and to the possibility of reconnection, in whatever form that may take. May you find peace within yourself, and may you never forget the love that once bound us together. No matter where life takes you, you are forever a part of my heart.

I release you now, not because I want to, but because I know that love can never be forced or bound by expectations. I release my hopes, my dreams, and my desire for the future into the universe, trusting that whatever happens, the love between us will remain sacred and eternal.

Until we meet again—whether in this life or the next—I carry you with me always.

With all my love,

[Your Name] (Grandparent)

Reinforcing that Love, Even from Afar, Is Still Real and Sacred

Even though you may not be in direct contact with your grandchild, the love you hold for them is real and sacred. Love, by its nature, transcends physical boundaries. It isn't defined by the frequency of communication or the moments shared in person. Your love is a force that exists independent of estrangement. It is not diminished by absence, and it remains unshaken, a constant presence in your heart.

The bond between a grandparent and grandchild is unique—a love that is often rooted in generations of wisdom, unconditional care, and a deep, quiet understanding. It is a love that shapes who you are and who your grandchild becomes, even if they are far away. No amount of time, no distance, no silence can erase the fact that you once held each other's hearts in an unspoken way.

This love is sacred because it is pure, unconditional, and enduring. Even in the midst of estrangement, that sacred love is still there, unbroken and waiting. It is sacred because it is not dependent on circumstances; it exists because you care, because you have always cared, and because you always will.

Your grandchild may not realize it now, but the love you gave them is still a part of them. The memories, the lessons, and the values you shared will remain within them, a quiet part of their identity. Your love lives on in them, no matter how far apart you may be. You have planted seeds of love and care in their hearts, and while they may not be visible in the present, they remain, quietly waiting to bloom.

Embracing the Identity of a Grandparent, Regardless of Estrangement

Estrangement doesn't take away your identity as a grandparent. Being a grandparent is not a role that is solely defined by your relationship with your grandchildren. It is an identity rooted in love, wisdom, and the ability to nurture the next generation. Even if your grandchild is not physically present in your life right now, you are still a grandparent. Your capacity to love, to teach, and to give remains within you. That role is part of who you are, and it cannot be erased by estrangement.

In embracing this identity, you honor the love and legacy that you have built, even in the absence of the relationship you once had with your grandchild. You continue to be a grandparent in the truest sense—not because of the circumstances of the estrangement, but because of the love you still carry for them and the wisdom you have to offer.

Being a grandparent is not about having regular visits or playing a traditional role—it is about the love you give, the life lessons you impart, and the wisdom you carry with you. Even if you are not actively involved in your grandchild's life, you can still carry the identity of a grandparent with pride and dignity. You are a part of a generational thread, and that thread will continue to weave through the lives of those you love, regardless of the distance.

Conclusion

The relationship between a grandparent and grandchild is one of love, wisdom, and shared experiences. Even when estrangement creates a painful separation, the love you hold for your grandchild remains real and sacred. A closing letter or blessing is a way to honor that love, to express your feelings and hopes, and to release the weight of the past while still holding on to the love that endures.

No matter where life takes you or your grandchild, the love between you is unbroken. You are still a grandparent, regardless of the estrangement. The love, the wisdom, and the legacy you've shared cannot be erased. It is a part of who you are, and it will forever remain with your grandchild, even in their absence.

The journey of estrangement may be filled with pain and uncertainty, but by embracing the love you hold and acknowledging your identity as a grandparent, you honor the bond that will never fade. Whether through a letter, a blessing, or simply holding them in your heart, the love you have for your grandchild is eternal, and that is a beautiful, sacred truth.

BONUS SECTION (OPTIONAL): RESOURCES FOR HEALING

Navigating the emotional journey of estrangement as a grandparent can be incredibly challenging, but it's important to remember that you don't have to go through it alone. There are many resources available that can provide support, guidance, and healing as you process your grief and work toward reconnection or acceptance. Below, we've compiled a list of recommended books, support groups, online forums, letter-writing prompts, affirmations, and guided meditations to help you on your healing journey.

Recommended Books for Grandparents in Grief

1. **"The Grandparent's Guide to Estrangement" by Dr. Lillian Glass** This book provides a compassionate and insightful look at estrangement from the perspective of grandparents. It offers strategies for coping, understanding, and potentially reconnecting with estranged grandchildren. Dr. Glass explores the emotional and psychological dynamics of estrangement and offers practical advice for healing.

2. **"The Invisible String" by Patrice Karst** A children's book that offers a beautiful metaphor for the enduring connection between people, even when separated by

distance. While not specifically for grandparents, this book can help children understand and process emotional separation and might provide a meaningful way to explain the concept of love that transcends distance.

3. **"Healing the Heart of Your Grandchild" by Dr. David Code** This book offers insights into how grandparents can support their grandchildren emotionally, even from a distance. It discusses ways in which grandparents can help their grandchildren heal from emotional wounds, whether or not the grandparent is actively involved in their life.

4. **"Surviving the Emotional Trauma of Estrangement" by Mark Sichel** Mark Sichel, a family therapist, offers advice on how to heal after emotional trauma, including estrangement. This book provides practical steps to help those affected by family estrangement regain their emotional equilibrium.

Support Groups for Estranged Grandparents

1. **Grandparents' Support Group (Facebook)** This online Facebook group offers a space for estranged grandparents to connect, share their experiences, and support each other. It's a safe and private community where you can ask for advice, find comfort in others' stories, and receive emotional support.

2. **The Estranged Grandparent Support Group (Online Forum)** A private online forum dedicated to helping estranged grandparents heal. The group allows members to share their experiences anonymously, seek guidance, and receive peer support from others facing similar challenges.

3. **ElderCare and Support Groups (AARP)** The AARP offers support for older adults and their families, including information on estrangement. AARP's resources can help you navigate your role as an elder in your family, providing helpful advice and support for those dealing with estrangement or loss.

4. **National Alliance for Grieving Children (NAGC)** This organization offers resources and support for grieving children and families. While not specifically focused on estrangement, NAGC can provide valuable insights on helping children cope with emotional loss and estrangement.

Online Forums for Estranged Grandparents

1. **Grandparents Coping with Estrangement (Reddit)** Reddit hosts a variety of support communities, including a subreddit for grandparents navigating estrangement. This online space allows you to ask questions, share experiences, and receive advice from others who understand the emotional complexity of estrangement.

2. **Estranged Parents & Grandparents Support Forum (Family Estrangement Forums)** This online forum allows grandparents and parents to share their stories of estrangement. It includes sections for emotional support, resources for reconnection, and discussions about how to cope with the pain of family distance.

Letter-Writing Prompts for Grandparents

Writing letters can be a therapeutic way to express your feelings, whether or not they are ever sent. Below are some prompts to help guide your letter-writing process, allowing you to express the love and emotions that you may have difficulty verbalizing otherwise.

1. A Letter of Love and Blessing

- Write a letter to your grandchild that expresses the love you have for them, your memories together, and the hopes you have for their future.

- "Even though we are apart, I want you to know how much I love you. I think about you every day and cherish the memories we made together..."

2. A Letter of Healing and Understanding

- Write a letter acknowledging the estrangement, expressing your sadness, but also showing understanding and compassion for their perspective.

- "I understand that things between us changed, and I'm sorry for the pain it caused. I wish I could understand better, but I want you to know I respect your feelings..."

3. A Letter of Hope

- Write a letter filled with hope for the future, whether or not a reunion is possible.

- "No matter what happens, my heart will always hold a place for you. I hope that one day we can reconnect, but even if not, I'll always hold you in my heart."

4. A Letter of Forgiveness

- Write a letter forgiving yourself or your family for what happened and release the weight of guilt.

- "I forgive myself for any mistakes I may have made, and I forgive the circumstances that led us here. I understand now that the past cannot be changed, but I carry forward only love..."

Affirmations for Grandparents in Grief

Affirmations can help shift your mindset and foster healing. Here are a few affirmations specifically for grandparents dealing with estrangement and grief:

1. "I am worthy of love, regardless of the circumstances."

2. "My love for my grandchild is unconditional and eternal."

3. "I release guilt and embrace peace within myself."

4. "I trust that healing is possible, even if it takes time."

5. "I am not defined by estrangement; I am defined by my capacity to love."

6. "I have the strength to endure and heal through this process."

7. "I will continue to love, even from a distance, and that love is enough."

8. "I trust that I am capable of rebuilding my life, with or without reconciliation."

Guided Meditations for Grandparents in Grief

Meditation can be an incredibly healing practice for those navigating grief and estrangement. Here are a few guided meditation practices you can try:

1. Loving-Kindness Meditation

- Focus on sending love to yourself and your grandchild, even from a distance. This meditation helps release any resentment or sadness, replacing it with compassion and forgiveness.

- "May I be happy, may I be at peace. May my grandchild be happy, may they be at peace."

2. Grief and Healing Meditation

- A guided meditation focused on allowing grief to flow and be processed. It can help release pent-up emotions, bringing a sense of calm and acceptance to the heart.
- "With every breath, I release the sadness and invite healing and peace into my heart."

3. Mindfulness of the Present

- Focus on being present in the moment, embracing the now and releasing the attachment to outcomes. This meditation helps ease anxiety about the future and fosters a sense of peace.
- "In this moment, I am whole, I am at peace, and I am enough."

4. Gratitude Meditation

- A meditation to focus on the things you are grateful for, shifting your focus away from what is absent and onto the blessings you still have.
- "I am grateful for the love I have given, the love I have received, and the memories I carry forward."

Conclusion

Estrangement from a grandchild is a deeply emotional journey, but you don't have to walk it alone. Whether you find support through books, online communities, support groups, or personal practices like letter writing and meditation, healing is possible. By giving yourself permission to grieve, heal, and find new ways to express your love, you open yourself up to possibilities for emotional growth, peace, and even reconnection. Remember that while the road may be difficult, you are stronger than you think, and the love you carry will always be a part of who you are.

CONCLUSION

The Grandchild I Hold in My Heart

As we come to the end of this journey, it's important to remember that the love you have for your grandchild is not diminished by distance or silence. Throughout this book, we have explored the complex and often silent grief of estranged grandparents, but we have also embraced the hope, healing, and potential for renewal that exists within you. The love you hold for your grandchild is sacred, and it remains an integral part of who you are, no matter the state of the relationship.

Estrangement is a painful reality, one that can leave you feeling isolated, unheard, and uncertain of the future. But through every chapter of this book, you've learned to process your grief, unpack the complex emotions of guilt and self-blame, and find meaningful ways to cope with the uncertainty that comes with estrangement. You've explored the possibility of reconnecting, but also learned to embrace a new relationship with hope—one that does not depend on a specific outcome but allows you to reclaim your joy, identity, and peace in the present moment.

The journey toward healing, as we've seen, is not one of quick fixes or perfect resolutions. It is a slow, often painful, but ultimately empowering process. And it's important to remember that you are not alone. There are countless other grandparents who share in your grief, your longing, and your hope. Through the support of communities, online forums, and therapy, you can continue to heal and find strength in the stories of others who have walked the same path.

By becoming mentors, surrogate grandparents, or community elders, you have the opportunity to love outward when your own love feels blocked. You can continue to give from the well of love within you, nurturing the younger generation while also nurturing yourself. This new role can help bring healing, joy, and a sense of purpose into your life, even as you wait, hope, or decide to let go of the estranged relationship.

In the end, the love you have for your grandchild—whether they are near or far, whether they come back or not—is never lost. It exists in your heart, always. This book has been an invitation to honor that love, to release the weight of the past, and to embrace a future filled with possibility, regardless of the outcomes.

And so, the final blessing to your grandchild is one of hope, peace, and unyielding love. Whatever the future holds, may you continue to carry the identity of a grandparent with pride, joy, and unconditional love. The bond you share with your grandchild, regardless of estrangement, will always remain a part of your heart—sacred, real, and eternal. You are, and will always be, the grandparent they hold in their heart.

www.ingramcontent.com/pod-product-compliance
Lightning Source LLC
Chambersburg PA
CBHW071528120626
46550CB00006B/2390

* 9 7 8 1 9 6 9 7 0 3 2 1 8 *